T[ ] ( ] Zen Grove

Phrases for Zen Practice

SECOND EDITION,
Expanded, Revised, Corrected and Reset

with Japanese Translations and Commentaries by
Shibayama Zenkei Rōshi
Late Abbot, Nanzen-ji, Kyōto, Japan and Kanchō of the Nanzenji-ha

and Selected by
Shimano Eidō Rōshi
Abbot of Dai Bosatsu Zendo Kongō-ji, New York State
and of New York Zendo Shōbō-ji, New York City

English Translation and Editing by
Zenrin Chidō Robert E. Lewis

Distributed by
THE ZEN STUDIES SOCIETY PRESS

Jacksonville
ZEN SANGHA PRESS
1996

Zen Sangha Press
7405 Arlington Expressway
Jacksonville, FL 32211-5999
(904) 721-1050   fax (904) 725-8561

Second Edition
Printed in the United States of America
on acid-free paper.

Distributed by
The Zen Studies Society Press
H.C.R. #1, Box 171
Livingston Manor, NY 12758-9732
(914) 439-4566   fax (914) 439-3119

Library of Congress Catalog Card Number: 96-60319
Hardcover ISBN: 0-9651499-2-7
Softcover ISBN: 0-9651499-3-5

To

Nyogen Senzaki

1876 - May 7, 1958

(In America, 1905-1958)

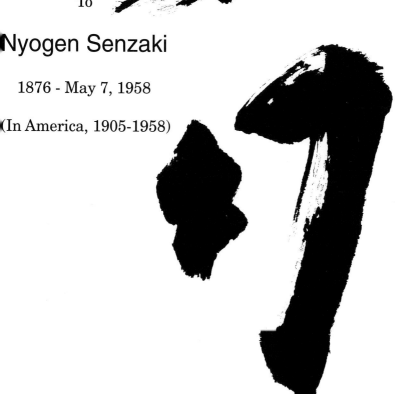

The characters read: *Nyo gen* "Like a Fantasy" (from Diamond 32).
The calligraphy is by Eido Roshi.

CONTENTS

INTRODUCTION

What Rinzai had—arms, legs, a head, nose and eyes . . . and what he saw—trees through the window . . . and what he did—walking, standing, sitting . . . is just what we have, what we see and what we do. There are differences, but fundamentally our experience—a thousand years later—is his experience: We face what he faced. And so what he said about life is about our modern American life—our lives.

Each phrase of the *Zenrin Kushu*, whether it is long or short, is the expression of enlightenment itself. It is beyond space and time and culture and language. As Buddhism moves to the West, it is natural to have an English *Zenrin Kushu*. In this sense this book is not a mere translation, but a newly created, newly compiled, Twentieth Century *Zenrin Kushu*. In fact, we could add some verses from sources like the Bible, Shakespeare and Dostoevsky. Suppose we find in the future *Zenrin Kushu* a phrase:

> To be or not to be—that is the question.
>
> (Hamlet 3155)

—that has the same impact as one of the Chinese phrases but is not strange at all to American ears.

Shibayama Zenkei Roshi's *Zenrin Kushu* [ZRKS in the bibliography] has never been translated by Western students of the Dharma or scholars into any European language. This work is unprecedented and it has its own value, but, like everything else, the pioneer work has to be carried on by following generations. Someone has to start with great difficulty. What the reader will see in this translation is the outcome of Zenrin Bob Lewis' amazing effort.

When he came to Dai Bosatsu Zendo for the first time, he mentioned that he was working on translating the ZRKS. I was surprised to learn that this stranger even knew of the existence of ZRKS. When he said that he was translating it, that went beyond being surprising. But I had an intuition: "Perhaps he *can* do it." I was not too attached to my wish, though, having had long experience with the impermanence and unpredictability of human life.

And then there was another surprise. He quit his job and came to Dai Bosatsu Zendo as a Kessei student. So, gradually, we began talking about and selecting the phrases. We sat together, and I marked my selections of the famous phrases, a few pages at a time.

I deliberately took the Zen style of teaching: I did not teach—I left it up to him to find his own way. It was like the Chinese saying, "The lion parents kick their cubs over the cliff, and only if the cub climbs back up is he worthy to train."

He copied each phrase onto an index card, looked things up in dictionaries and made his own translations. By doing so, he "climbed up the cliff". It was then that I realized that he was seriously willing to take on the task. So I decided to help him in any way I could.

With some doubtful translations, there was no problem; with others, because of his training in the sciences and mine in Japanese and Chinese literature, the East-West communications problems rose to meet us. But with much struggle, we came to understand each other's approach.

It was in the summer of 1980 that the readiness of time brought him to decide to become a Rinzai Zen monk. I had no hesitation to give him the Dharma name Zenrin. In fact, there is no other name for him.

As I said before, each phrase of the ZRKS, long or short, is the expression of enlightenment. In the Japanese Rinzai Zen tradition, when a student has studied a koan under his teacher's guidance and he "passes" that koan, the teacher asks him to bring a *jakugo*. The use of *jakugo* and the purpose of this unique study is well expressed by Ruth Sasaki in *Zen Dust*:

> . . . when the student had satisfied the master as to his understanding of a koan, he was asked to bring to the master a line or two in verse or prose which . . . summarized the import of the koan. The capping phrase was not to be original with the student; it was to be a quotation taken from the literature, preferably secular, of any period. *Zenrin Kushu*, an anthology of quotations from Chinese and Japanese sources compiled shortly before Hakuin's time, with which he is said to have become acquainted in his youth, was the principal source for these *jakugo*.

The student has no other way but to look in the ZRKS again and again, until he has almost memorized everything. The teacher does not give any explicit clue, but patiently waits. In this training system, we can see the typical Oriental approach to learning. Once in a while, however, the teacher, in a very subtle way, gives the student a hint.

I remember when I was working on a certain koan. My teacher, Nakagawa Soen Roshi, asked me to bring a *jakugo*. I searched in the ZRKS, and brought what I had found, and all were rejected, one after the other, dokusan after dokusan. [Dokusan is private interview with the master.] Months passed. I searched through the ZRKS again and again. One day, my teacher was changing a scroll in front of me, and what it said on that scroll was it! So I smiled and said, "You are too subtle." And he said, "Did you get it?" And I said, "I got it. Thank you very much!"

Though this is a rather unusual happening, koan study in the Rinzai Zen tradition gives the student the opportunity—more than an opportunity, a pressure—to read, learn and even memorize the Chinese classics. As the context in which Zen literature was created was the culture of the Tang Dynasty in China, total familiarity is extremely helpful to grasp the vital spirit of Zen.

However, this is the 20th Century American ZRKS, a ground-breaking work. The monastery must be built on it. It is my sincere hope that readers of this ZRKS will not only read this collection repeatedly, but that they will also be inspired by these sayings to do more and stronger zazen practice—to realize their own true nature.

Eido Tai Shimano
Dai Bosatsu Zendo
July 4, 1984

PREFACE

Browse! —you may happen on what you're looking for. The concordance at the end will help you refind a phrase by way of its images, almost all of them familiar and natural. And if your determination to meditate doesn't coalesce, try a phrase—dipping into the phrases again after sitting, with deepened insight.

The rest of this preface can wait.

The Zen Grove. The grove of trees stands for a community of monks, non-dependent like the free-standing pines and ongoing as a community down the generations [see phrases #460, #525 and #605]. The phrases translated here are selected from ZRKS [see p. 117], whose title translates as "The Zen Grove's Phrase Collection". "Book of the Zen Grove" because Rinzai Zen monks keep this book handy to dip into in free moments, and so get the phrases by heart.

The Phrases in English—How to Find Them. Each phrase was translated anew from the Chinese original into colloquial American English, even vulgar slang when the intent of the phrase seemed best conveyed in such terms. The result was checked against Zenkei Roshi's Japanese translation and commentary and also the existing English translations of its source [see p. 108-115], as well as the phrase collections in CY, ZD and DCZ [p. 116-117]. (It was the deeply beautiful translations of Sokei-an in CY that first inspired me to attempt to translate from ZRKS.) The translations are fairly literal, sometimes even keeping to the order of the Chinese characters of the original phrase. This is possible because Zenkei Roshi's commentary usually heads off possible misunderstanding; in other cases, a brief explanation in brackets is added to the commentary.

The Concordance at the back of the book also serves as a topical index—of phenomena much more than of abstract ideas—to the phrases.

The Original Chinese Phrases and Their Arrangement. Except for phrases taken from more ancient sources: the sutras, the *Dao De Jing* and Confucius—their vocabulary is, literally, natural, and their grammar, in the main, straightforward. So, with the close interlinear English translations, this book can be used as a beginning "classical" (or "Zen") Chinese-English reader. Those phrases that are two (or four) lines of equal length [p. 60-107] have, almost without exception, the strict and strongly subtle parallelism-and-contrast characteristic of the poetry of the Tang.

The phrases are grouped in sections by length, and, within each section, "by radicals". These 部首 *bushu*, "radicals," or, more correctly, "significs," are characters occurring within all others, one in each, that classify them and suggest their meanings, much as shop signs once pictured something of the wares inside. The dictionary N is arranged by significs; M has a signific index; and SH is by stroke count, then by significs. The great advantage of the significs—standardized in China around 1700—is that they are independent of dialect. The mnemonic for the significs (inside the back and front covers) lists them in order. [Some have abbreviations, used when they occur in other characters; these are given after their full forms in brackets.] Each signific is followed by one of its definitions in **boldface**, the whole mnemonic forming a kind of poem.

The Japanese Translations. Zenkei Roshi translated the original phrases into *bungo*: literary Japanese—a concise and elegant written language (conveniently covered in H). The Japanese translations of Zenkei Roshi are given here, romanized, directly under the original Chinese.

Occasionally they vary from those in ZRKS—because I have followed Eido Roshi wherever he chose a different rendering.

Use of the Symbols in the Japanese Translations.

Japanese word order is markedly different from that of Chinese (and English)—the most striking difference being that the verb comes at the end of the phrase in Japanese. This rearrangement is indicated by symbols in the romanized Japanese translations: Subscripts "$_x$, $_1$, $_2$, $_3$, ..." between words and the marks "|, (, [,]" within words are there to show how to find out which Japanese syllables are readings or translations of a given *kanji* [Japanese for a Chinese character] in the original phrase.

To find the romanized Japanese syllable used to pronounce each *kanji*, we isolate and rearrange them in the order of the *kanji* in the original Chinese:

> (1) Delete every hyphen along with the following [apparent] word [: followed by a space].

> (2) Rearrange strings of [apparent] words [: between spaces] with numerical subscripts into the order of their subscripts, interchange words with the subscript "$_x$" between, and delete all subscripts.

> (3) If a word contains a left bracket "["— move the bracket, together with the word ending after it, in front of the rest of the original word as a new, separate word.

> (4) Delete each word ending that follows a left parenthesis "(".

> (5) Delete each vertical line "|".

The resulting words are in the same order as their corresponding *kanji* in the original Chinese phrase.

For example,

禍不入愼家門

(5) Wazawai [zu i(shin ka mon.
(4) Wazawai [zu i(shin|ka mon.
(3) Wazawai [zu i(ra shin|ka mon.
(2) Wazawai i(ra[zu shin|ka mon.
(1) Wazawai   shin|ka $_2$ mon $_3$ i(ra[zu$_1$.
249. Wazawai-wa shin|ka-no$_2$ mon-ni$_3$ i(ra[zu$_1$.

好雪片片不落別處

(5) Kō setsu hem pen [zu o(bes sho.
(4) Kō|setsu hem|pen [zu o(bes|sho.
(3) Kō|setsu hem|pen [zu o(chi bes|sho.
(2) Kō|setsu hem|pen o(chi[zu bes|sho.
(1) Kō|setsu hem|pen bcs|sho $_x$ o(chi[zu.
380. Kō|setsu hem|pen bes|sho-ni $_x$ o(chi[zu.

The Linguistic Significance of These Symbols. Written Japanese was adapted from Chinese in two ways:

1. *Onyomi*. Words, "clusters," were composed of *kanji*, each *kanji* being pronounced with its Chinese meaning and sound (in some Chinese dialect of that time and as approximated with a native Japanese syllable). This is a "reading by sound," Japanese *onyomi*. In the romanized Japanese translations given here, the sounds of the *kanji* in these clusters are divided within the word by vertical lines "|".

2. *Kunyomi* "reading by meaning": A *kanji* is used to write the beginning of a native Japanese word of nearly the same meaning, and the rest of the word, its ending, which will take different forms depending on the word's grammatical function, is written in *kana*, the Japanese phonetic symbols [themselves simplified *kanji*]. (*Kana* are introduced in the first eight lessons of RJ and discussed in Appendix 7 of N.) Romanized here, the first part of the word is divided from the ending by a left parenthesis. Note that "a(u" [as in #562] and "o(u" [as in #531] are both pronounced "ō".

Subscripts. The subscript "$_x$" between two romanized Japanese words means that in the Chinese the two *kanji* clusters and/or *kunyomi-kanji* occurred in the reverse order. Numerical subscripts to a string of Japanese words mean that in the Chinese the corresponding *kanji* clusters and/or *kunyomi-kanji* were in the order of the subscripts.

Hyphens. A Japanese particle, also called a postposition (that connects the word it follows with another word, as our preposition does the word it precedes), is written in *kana*. Romanized here, a hyphen joins the particle to the word it follows.

Brackets. Sometimes a *kanji* prefixed to another in the Chinese, particularly if the former is a negative, is translated with a Japanese grammatical word-ending in *kana*. Romanized here, this ending is divided from the rest of the word by a left bracket "[".

Kanji translated with *kana*. When a *kanji* is translated with a native Japanese word in *kana*, its romanization is enclosed in brackets "[ ]".

For reading and writing *kana* and beginning *kanji*, see RJ. The historical development of written Japanese is traced in R.A. Miller's *The Japanese Language* (University of Chicago Press, 1967), Chapter 3: Writing Systems—and that of the *onyomi* in B. Karlgren's *Grammata Serica* (Stockholm: Bulletin of the Museum of Far Eastern Antiquities, No. 12, 1940; Taipei: Ch'eng-wen Publishing Company, 1968), p. 65-89: Ancient Chinese and Sino-Japanese.

The Japanese index is taken from ZRKS. In it the original phrases are read vertically, then right-to-left. The order is, first by the number of kanji in the phrase, then by an onyomi (there are usually more than one for a single *kanji*) of the first *kanji* in the phrase in the Japanese "50-syllable phonetic alphabet" (which is given in RJ and N).

Sources and Acknowledgments. The lists of English translations that follow some of the sources in the bibliography have a dual purpose: Firstly, they can be used to become more familiar with the text a *teisho* (Zen discourse) is to be on by finding the phrases in this book—with their commentaries—that occur in that text. Secondly, one can use them to critically compare the various translations of a given source by comparing some of the famous phrases here as translated in each. Though translations of Zen texts vary widely in style and quality, you can determine which of them to rely on. One can even go back to the original of a favorite phrase and get a sense of its meaning with the help of dictionaries—and then look at the form it takes in the various translations from *that* point of view.

This book, and especially the bibliography, is open-ended: Because the phrases were finished first, the citations in them (in parentheses) to the sources are less complete than the citations in the bibliography back to the phrases; UA is a "principal source" that did not arrive in time to be included in that section, so it is under "other sources"; because quite a few "other sources," like the "principal sources" a generation or two ago, are practically unknown in English, the citations to them are sometimes nonspecific and incomplete.

Zen translations into English are not at all a closed corpus. If the long-ago process of the translation of Sanskrit Buddhist texts into Chinese is any indication, the struggle for accurate completeness is likely to go on for centuries to come.

This book was possible because Eido Roshi was willing to select the most famous phrases in ZRKS for translation. He found time to help with his knowledge of Zen idioms and Tang poetry when something—something—was wrong with my translation of a phrase, and also when I had missed subtleties in the Japanese of a commentary. Most helpful was his insistence that I understand a phrase—not just translate it. Thanks also to Eido Roshi for little-known data on the lineage [facing p. 1]. Here only Dharma heirs (of Hakuin Zenji, and, ultimately, Shakyamuni Buddha) are included, so some Zen *Bodhisattva-mahasattva*s who lived and worked in America—notably D.T. Suzuki and Nyogen Senzaki—don't appear. For the rest of the lineage and those of other schools of Zen Buddhism, see ZD, p. 487-510, and [far more complete, but *kanji*-only] ZGD, volume III, section 2.

Thanks also to Kichudo of Kyoto for permission to use the phrases in Chinese for the Japanese index; to the late Mrs. Mary Farkas for permission to use the quotation from ZD in the Introduction; to Prof. Masatoshi Nagatomi for help with the bibliography (but errors of omission and commission are my own); to my late father, Edward J. Lewis, for something of the art of printing; to Saman Sodo Lea Liu, for the time and energy she devoted to prepublication drafts and much more; to Frank Hanisko, to Leslie Palmer and especially to Oscar Senn for great help with scanning and laser printing; to the Obaku Zen priest Daiho Hirose for help with Zen terminology and texts; to Prof. John C. Maraldo for loaning valuable reference works; to Thomas Kirchner for pointing out errors and awkwardnesses in my phrase translations; to Richard Vach for proofreading; to Jiro Andy Afable for his accurate ear; to Genro Lee Milton, for publishing excerpts; to Robert C. Broward, A.I.A., for the Jacksonville places of publication; and to Mr. and Mrs. C.F. Carlson, for Xerography and The Workplace!

Zenrin R. Lewis
Dai Bosatsu Mountain,
September 15, 2447 [=CE 1984];
Kichu-an,
July 4, 2459 [=CE 1996]

Rinzai Zen Transmission Into the United States

Family name and Dharma name are given for living masters, Dharma name and monk's name for others. Names of those who came to America are in italics, *but in* **boldface** *if they stayed.*

The Buddha (April 8, 463 - Feb. 15, 383 BCE) —⫻— Bodhidharma (? - Oct. 5, 532)
[Buddha Shākyamuni, Gautama Siddhartha]   [Daruma Daishi]

臨濟義玄
Rinzai Gigen (? - April 10, 866) —⫻— Hakuin Ekaku (1685 - Dec. 11, 1768)
[Línjì Yìxuán]   白隱慧鶴

峨山慈棹
Gasan Jitō (1726-1797)

妙喜宗績   迦陵瑞迦   潭海玄昌
Myōki Sōseki (1774-1848)-Karyō Zuika (1790-1859)-Tankai Genshō (1811-1898)

毒湛匝三   霧海古亮   來山泰祐
Dokutan Sōsan (1840-1917)-Mukai Koryō (1864-1935)-Kyōsan Taiyū (1886-1954)
[Nakamura Taiyū]

卓州胡僊   一舟慈棹
Takujū Kosen (1760-1833)   **Isshū Jitō** (1903 - Dec. 10, 1978)
[Miura Isshū]

蘇山玄喬   伽山全楞   宗般玄芳
Sozan Genkyō (1798-1866)-Kasan Zenryo (1824-1893)-Sōhan Gempō (1848-1922)

玄峯宜雄   宋淵玄珠
Gempō Giyū (1865-1961)—*Sōen Genju* (1907 - March 11, 1984)
[Yamamoto Gempō]   [Nakagawa Sōen]

嶋野榮道
Shimano Eidō (1932 -
[Muishitsu Eidō]

儀山善來   洪川宗溫
Gisan Zenrai (1802-1878)—Kōsen Sōon (1816-1892)
[Imakita (or Imagita) Kōsen]

洪嶽宗演   輟翁宗活
Kōgaku Sōen (1859 - Nov. 1, 1919)—*Tetsuō Sōkatsu* (1870-1954)
[Shaku Sōen, Soyen Shaku]   [Sōkatsu Shaku]

指月宗岑
Shigetsu Sōshin (1882 - May 17, 1945)
[Sasaki Shigetsu, Sōkei-an]

隱山惟琰   太元孜元
Inzan Ien (1751-1814)—Taigen Shigen (1768-1837)

大拙承演   獨園承珠
Daisetsu Jōen (1797-1855)—Dokuon Jōshu (1818-1895)

盤龍禪楚   承天宗杲
Banryō Zenso (1848-1936)—Jōten Sōkō (1871-1958)
[Miura Jōten]

佐々木承周
Sasaki Jōshū (1907 -
[Kyōzan Jōshū]

ONE

了 **1. Ryō!** (Zen 12)

That's it! Finished, settled, completely understanding. The end. "That's it!" means that insight is already attained, and "Not yet!" that insight is yet to be attained.

參 **2. San.** (Comprehensive 14; Daie)

Go see. At the end of a Dharma talk, "go see" means to meditate deeply on it. And when a student is received intimately in the master's room to cultivate himself in the Buddha's Way, it means to go and find out, to go and ask, etc.

叱 **3. Shitsu!** (Realm 2)

Ass! A scolding and abusive shout. "Shitsu! Shitsu!" is a stinging rebuke. Scold severely.

吽 **4. Un!** (Rinzai 2XIII)

Moo! The sound of the lowing of an ox. It expresses a wonderful truth that's beyond words.

咦 **5. Ii!** (Mu 41C)

Ii! A sigh of admiring wonder, implying something that will never get an explanation in words. Taking it literally, as an exclamation of surprise and censure, doesn't penetrate to this "something".

喏 **6. Daku.** (Mu 12K)

Yes. A response: The "yes" of compliance.

唯 **7. Ii!**

Hai! The sound of the reply "Hai!" [= "Yes!" in Japanese]. Even more than "Daku," it's a courteous reply—and a solid affirmation.

喝 **8. Katsu!!!** (Rinzai Preface, 1I,IV,V, 2I,II,IV,IX,X,XIV,XX,XXI,XXIII, 3I,XIII,XXI)

Gkhaught!!! This character stands for an intensely vehement shout, a Zen action that gives expression to the state of enlightenment—hard to manifest. It can also be a severely scolding cry to train the student. The cry that bursts through, that says it all!

噫 **9. I!** (Cliff 51K)

Alas! A sigh "Ah—" of lamentation and an exclamation of surprise, dismay and censure.

囚

10. Ka! (Cliff 66K)

Ho!

A spontaneous shout, the exclamation of great enlightenment. Also, the cry when grappling a ship. ([The tea master] Sen no Rikyū pronounced it as "I" in his death poem, referring to a "three-character poem" [of Ummon].)

寂

11. Jaku.

Tranquil.

Being quiet, a sense of calm aloneness. And, bound for Nirvāna, all lusts and passions cut away, the state of enlightened peace and quiet, soothing and bracing.

放

12. Hō. (Mu 15K)
Release
from.

To pardon, spare, set free.

是

13. Ze! (Cliff 38K)
Right,
it's this!

Good! Well done! Perfect!—with a sense of agreement and direct, immediate affirmation.

無

14. Mu! (Mu 1K)

Mu!

Jōshū expressed our innate Buddha-nature in a word: "Mu" [literally, "not, without"]. The subtle sense of enlightenment that goes beyond "is" and "not".

然

15. Zen.

Really.

A word used to confide in someone in good faith: Indeed, thus—etc. Word of honor.

看

16. Kan! (Cliff 62I,V)
Look!

Shading your eyes with your hand, look carefully. See. Pay attention.

漸耳

17. Nii! (Equanimity 64K; Mu 12C)

Nii!

There! Look! . . . A word of direct pointing that demands total attention to an implied meaning. (This character "Nii," written on a piece of paper kept pasted over a door, is intended to drive evil spirits and malevolent demons thousands of miles away—a practice adopted from China.)

夢

18. Mu. (Cliff 40K)

Dream.

The empty transiency of things—that melt away in a moment. It also indicates the state of freedom from thoughts and desires. Aspirations painting the future.

19. Zoku! (Rinzai 2V,VII)
Thief!
A term for the Zen adept, admiring his excellence of action, as being like the cunning of a thief. *Not* terrible negligence. [Literally, robber, rebel, traitor.]

20. Shaku. (Cliff 98K,V)
Wrong.
An error. You're making a mistake!—acting unreasonably.

21. Kan. (Rinzai Preface)
Calm.
What even the Buddhas and Patriarchs couldn't figure out, the tranquil state when even enlightenment's grime is cut and gone. Leisure inconspicuous and serene, the opposite of busyness.

22. Katsu. (Eye)
Distance.
Generosity of spirit, immensity, distant coolness, willingness to let acquaintances lapse, magnanimity . . . Limitless grandeur.

23. Kan. (Cliff 8K)
Barrier.
An absolute frontier, beyond delusion and enlightenment. A checkpoint you can't pass through recklessly. A barrier in the way of peace of mind.

24. A. [The first of the twelve vowels of the Siddhaṃ alphabet.]
A.
The Chinese character initially used for the first sound of the Japanese syllabary. It stands for the fundamental fact of birthlessness, for the root source of everything, for experiential absoluteness, and more. This character, having an unusual abundance of meanings, is not at all simple.

25. Ro! (Ummon)
Revealed!
As a Zen one-word barrier, it means: Look! Right before your eyes, revealing in splendor. It may be read "appear". As a Zen term, "dew; be wet"—other meanings of the character—don't apply.

26. Moku. (Vimalakīrti 9)
Silence.
With enlightenment's subtle taste, this doesn't just mean wordlessness. The silence like silent thunder.

Two

不了　27. Fu|ryō.　(Rinzai 1XIV,XIX,XX)
　　　　　　(You) imperfectly understand—haven't finished.
[You're] not done!

不審　28. Fu|shin.　(Rinzai 1II,2XVI)
How do
you do?
　　　　An expression of greeting: "How are you?" Or, "Oh! How nice!" (of
　　　　a gift). Also read as, "Astonishing, amazing!"

不會　29. Fu|e.　(Cliff 18K)
　　　　　　I don't see, can't figure it out; I'm not convinced.
I don't understand.

不識　30. Fu|shiki.　(Cliff 1K,V)
There's no
telling.
　　　　The idea is not that there must be understanding with knowledge.
　　　　There is no knowing. Implied is the idea that non-discrimination is
　　　　most intimate. ["Telling": Discriminative knowing.]

不道　31. I(wa[ji.　(Cliff 55K)
　　　　　　I won't say. I absolutely will never say!
I won't tell you.

了了　32. Ryō|ryō.　(Huáng-bò I32,35, II26)
Know for
sure.
　　　　· *Clearly* realize. It has the sense of explicit, decisive insight.

什麼　33. Na|n-zo.　(Lamp 5; Rinzai 1XVIIIa,c,d)
What!
　　　　Spoken frankly. Why? A word of doubt and question. Also read
　　　　"Jū|ma".

休去　34. Kyū-shi sa(ru.　(Mu 13K)
Let it rest,
dismiss.
　　　　Not caring for further discussion, cease and desist—meaning, part
　　　　for a pause.

作麼　35. So|mo.　(Rinzai 3XIII)
So?
　　　　Why? How? What? And read as, "What should I do?" [There's noth-
　　　　ing to do!]

別別 36. Betsu|betsu.　(Cliff 14V,100V)　　　　　　　　　　　　5

Now *this* is
something *else!*

Meaning, this is another matter, something further, something different.

勘破 37. Kam|pa.　(Cliff 4K,V)

Critical
examination.

Fathom the real situation and the true motives of others. See through.

呵呵 38. Ka|ka!

Ha-ha!

The hearty "Ha, ha!" when roaring laughter comes in bursts.

如是 39. Nyo|ze.　(Diamond 1)

Thus.

Right on this way; a true account as it stands. The Diamond Sutra begins, "Thus (have I heard)." And, words acknowledging another's interpretation.

恁麼 40. Im|mo.

Like this.

(How? . . .) Thus. This is it, this way . . . —affirming that something has been done.

更參 41. Sara-ni san(zeyo.　(Cliff 20V2n)

Practice
Further.

Still more, never enough—with this attitude be diligent in Zen practice.

未在 42. Mi|zai.

Not yet!

Still vain, useless, lacking integrity. (Said of an effort.)

無事 43. Bu|ji.　(Rinzai 1X,XIII,XVIIIa,d,h(twice),XX,XXII(thrice), 2VII)

Nothing-
doing.

Because there is no Buddha that is to be sought, reaching the sublime condition free of the idea that there is a Way that is to be followed, coming back to one's real Self, with the freedom of letting things take their natural course, the mind is at peace. [*Buji* is defined by D.T. Suzuki in note 7 to "Rinzai on Zen" in AZ.]

無我 44. Mu|ga.　(Diamond 14,23)

Anattā.

[A Pali word meaning "free of an ego or soul, selfless".] By getting rid of the idea that you have a [separate, fixed] self, the root of all your painful delusions, getting free of all attachments, you become completely adaptive and unrestricted.

6

無爲 45. Mu|i. (Song 1)
Without doings.
Giving up all attachments, live calmly.

珍重 46. Chin|chō. (Arsenal; Huáng-bò II26; Rinzai 1VII,XXII)
Take care!
A farewell expression wishing you a safe, happy journey and advising caution.

看看 47. Mi-yo mi-yo. (Cliff 62V; Rinzai 1III)
Look! Look!
Carefully, thoroughly look into.

知足 48. Chi|soku. (Dhammapada XV204)
Know when to stop.
Know contentment. Satisfied with one's station in life, not to stir up greedy thoughts. In the Dhammapada [Chapter XV, verse 204] there is: "Knowing when to stop is the greatest wealth."

知音 49. Chi|in. (Cliff 8I; Rinzai 3XII)
Know [his] sound.
Of friends whose minds are genuinely in communion and accord. A term taken from the Chinese tale [ZFZB I84]—about Bó-yá, an accomplished player of the qín [a kind of horizontal "guitar"]—and Zhōng-zi-qī, who was able to recognize the beautiful sound when he played.

與麼 50. Yo|mo. (Rinzai 1XVIIIc)
Such as this.
Like this. In that way. Also equivalent to "What!" and "So?".

那箇 51. Na|ko. (Rinzai 1II,3XII)
Which one?
(That, there, . . .) Which? —facing "THIS matter," the source of all things.

THREE

作什麼 52. Na|ni-o-ka ₓ na(su. (Rinzai 3VI)
Doing what?
What are you *doing?*

作麼生 53. So|mo|san. (Rinzai 2I,3IX)
What do *you* say?
How? How about it?

可惜許 54. Ka|shak|ko. (Cliff 23K)

Be sparing with acknowledgment!

It's too bad! What a pity [to say so]! "Ko" is a grammatical particle equivalent to "!".

惺惺著 55. Sei|sei|jaku. (Mu 12K)

Be mindful, alert!

Be clear-headed. "Jaku"—"be"—is an auxiliary character.

擔板漢 56. Tam|ban|kan. (Cliff 4Kn)

A board-carrying fellow.

A man fixed on one course. He sees only one side, as if carrying a plank on his shoulder. He's a slave to it, the same as a carriage horse.

放下著 57. Hō|ge|jaku. (5 Houses)

Drop it!

Your lot: On abandoned land, with men who've been let go. "Jaku" is an emphatic particle.

是什麼 58. Ko(re na|n-zo. (Cliff 51K)

What is THIS?!

Here, now, this—what *is* it?

未徹在 59. Mi|tetsu|zai. (5 Houses)

Not through To home.

Not yet penetrating through to enlightenment, still unsuccessful.

歸去來 60. Kaeri nan iza. (Cliff 51V)

Let's turn back home.

Let us return now, let us return!

沒交涉 61. Mok|kyō|shō. (Cliff 8Kc,47Kn)

Not relevant.

There's no connection at all. Lacking coherence, he can't even come close.

沒蹤跡 62. Motou|shō|ccki.

Not a trace.

Leaving no trail. The state of mind of emancipation, free of things like discrimination and attachment.

白拈賊 63. Byaku|nen|zoku. (Cliff 73V)

A thief snatching openly.

"Openly" means in broad daylight, and "snatching," stealing. Robbery in broad daylight—a fearsome deed. [See #19.]

8

看脚下 64. Kyak|ka-o$_x$ miyo.   (5 Houses)
Watch your   Be attentive to what's at your feet and be careful of your gait.
step!

瞎屡生 65. Katsu|ru|sei.   (Rinzai 1XVII and 1XVIIIi)
Blind   "Blind" means ignorant, and "again" implies folly. An abusive
again,   phrase aimed at an insensible fool.
dolt!

破草鞋 66. Ha|sō|ai.   (Cliff 19Vn; Realm 5:14)
     Straw sandals so torn they come off. Of what possible use are
Split   they?
straw sandals.

老古錐 67. Rō|ko|sui.
A solid,   A title of esteem for a master of surpassing Zen. Both "solid"
ancient   and "ancient" are terms of respect for mature perfection of
gimlet.   mind. Keeness of Zen-in-action is here spoken of figuratively as
     that of a gimlet. [See #626.]

莫妄想 68. Maku|mō|sō.
No more   Put an end to wild fancies. Never dwell on pointless rubbish.
delusive thinking.

落草談 69. Raku|sō-no dan.   (Cliff 34K)
Lose yourself   "Lose yourself in the weeds": Go down, even humble your
in the weeds   spirit, low in the weeds out of compassion—to teach and trans-
talking.   form beings. A Second-Principle Dharma talk—that being ex-
     pedient for their emancipation.

解打鼓 70. Kai|ta|ku.   (Cliff 44K)
Let loose on   The community a big drum is heard in. This drum is heard with
the drum.   the heart as well as the ear.

賊知賊 71. Zoku, zoku-o$_x$ shi(ru.   (Cliff 8Kn)
Thieves know   A snake *is* the path he takes. The best of friends, their minds
thieves.   in intimate accord. [See #19.]

遅八刻 72. Chi|hachi|koku.
Late eight   Already two whole hours late. Diffidence attacking the castle
quarter-   front gate! Being late with well-meant help.
hours.

那一人 73. Na|ichi|nin.
Who is he?
That unique person—the unconditioned True Self, the Original "Face".

那一曲 74. Na|ik|kyoku.
What is the tune?
That unique theme. What the Buddhas and Patriarchs said—as music. Enlightenment's subtle gist.

閑不徹 75. Kam|pu|tetsu. (Kidō 1)
Stillness everywhere, thorough silence.
Bar impenetrably.

閑葛藤 76. Kan|kat|tō.
Impeding, entangling creepers.
"Impeding" means useless. "Entangling creepers" are vines, ivy and lianas. They kill a huge tree by coiling round it. This refers to pointless writings that disturb practice.

露堂堂 77. Ro|dō|dō. (Jōwa 1)
Revealed in splendor!
Not a scene confronting you, boundless "splendor" comes in sight all around [like the halls and courts of an immense palace].

風顛漢 78. Fū|ten|kan. (Rinzai Preface, 2I)
A fool or crazy fellow.
A wind-blown-down fellow.

飯袋子 79. Han|tai|su. (Mu 15K)
Cooked-rice begging-bag master.
One subsisting on leftover cooked rice alone to help [the donors practice charity]. "This idler, so stingy he's grinding grain!"—is a rebuke for the feckless.

驀直去 80. Maku|jiki-ni sa(re. (Mu 31K)
Go right ahead.
Go at full speed—neither dropping your eyes nor looking aside: Don't start discriminating.

黒漫漫 81. Koku|mam|man. (Rinzai 1XXII)
Watchful darkness, waiting, completely in the dark.
Darkness deep and vast.

黒漆桶　82. Koku|shit|tsū.　(Cliff 86Kn)
A black
lacquer
pail.

A bucket lacquered black. Being completely black, it means pure and genuine, referring to the state of mind of "absolute equality" that goes beyond all relative distinctions.

FOUR

一刀兩斷
83. It|tō ryō|dan.　(Cliff 76Kn)

At one stroke, in two—cleft!

Cut off right-and-wrong and loss-and-gain with one blow.

一彩兩賽
84. Is|sai|ryō|sai.　(Rinzai 3VI)

The same color comes up on both dice.

Colors: Faces on dice. Two dice are thrown, and the same face comes up on both. These words convey the feeling of the superiority of two at once. Being two, one; being one, two. [In the *Rinzai Roku,* "is-" and "ryō" are interchanged: "Two colors on one die."]

一行三昧
85. Ichi|gyō zam|mai.　(Platform 14)

One-pointed samādhi.

With the mind straightforwardly concentrated, devoting undivided attention to each thing, worldly thoughts aren't generated—and, zazen.

七花八裂
86. Shik|ka hachi|retsu.　(Cliff 2Vn)

Seven flowers split into eight.

Meaning, become like bits of dust. The situation in which things go to pieces.

不昧因果
87. Fu|mai in|ga.　(Mu 2K)

Doesn't go against karma.

Doesn't deceive himself/others about the working of the law of causation—meaning: Karma being karma, he accepts that fact.

不生不死
88. Fu|shō fu|shi. (Nirvāṇa)

No birth, no death.

In great enlightenment there is no birth and death.

不落因果
89. Fu|raku in|ga. (Mu 2K)

Doesn't get caught up in karma.

This is freedom, unconstrained by the law of causation.

久立珍重
90. Kyū|ryū chin|chō. (Rinzai 1I,VI)

You've stood long; take care.

He makes an implied apology after expounding the Dharma before an assembly of monks, thanking them for listening attentively for so long.

佛祖乞命
91. Bus|so-mo mei-o_x ko(u. (Mu 43V)

[Even] the Buddhas and Patriarchs beg for their lives.

Enlightenment so point-blank that even the Buddhas and Patriarchs can't get near.

全提正令
92. Zen|tei shō|rei. (Mu 1V)

Completely manifest the true imperative.

The true imperative is the moral law, the Dharma taught by the Buddhas and the Patriarchs. This Dharma has been and is fully revealed.

再犯不容
93. Sai|bon yu(rusa[zu. (Cliff 38Kn; Rinzai 1IV)

The second time, the offense is unforgivable.

Let off once, the second time not!

冷暖自知
94. Rei|dan ji|chi. (Zen 16)

Cold and warmth you know yourself.

You can't understand water's coolness or warmth until you taste it yourself. In the same way, enlightenment has to be your own understanding, not the explanation of someone else.

12

函蓋乾坤

95. Kan|gai ken|kon.　(Cliff 14Kc)

[Like] box and cover, the sky and the ground.

As a box and its lid fit, and as the sky and the ground coincide at the horizon, so two persons accord perfectly, and the universe becomes one.

分疎不下

96. Bun|so fu|ge.　(Cliff 2Kc,11Kn,58K; Mu 19C)

It's inexplainable.

It's impossible to give a justification for it. Discernment is what is and has been needed.

前三後三

97. Zen|san go|san.　(Cliff 35K)

Before, three; behind, three.

A number that exceeds quantity as it's understood in this world. [Compare #224.]

劍刄上事

98. Ken|nin|jō-no ji.　(Rinzai 1VI)

The matter of the sword blade's edge.

Buddhism's vitally important matter is referred to as Zen enlightenment. To investigate this matter thoroughly you need a ready resolution to the death, as if walking a razor-sharp blade.

勘破了也

99. Kam|pa ryō|ya.　(Cliff 4K)

The critical examination is finished.

Saw through that and . . . "Not quite!" roars back.

千古無對

100. Sen|ko tai$_x$ na(shi.　(Cliff 8V)

Down through all the ages there's been no answer.

In essence it is beyond all contrasts, so words fall short.

千聖不傳

101. Sen|shō fu|den.　(Cliff 7I)

The thousands of sages haven't handed anything down.

All the Buddhas, past, present and future, and the successive generations of Patriarchs, are unable to teach others. Enlightenment has to be one's own experience.

千里同風

102. Sen|ri dō|fū.

For thousands of miles, it's the same wind.

Everywhere and right over *there*, it's the same.

即心即佛

103. Soku|shin soku|butsu.   (Mu 30K)

This very mind is the Buddha.

This mind, as it is, is the Buddha. Daibai asked, "What is the Buddha?" Baso said, "This very mind is the Buddha."

灰頭土面

104. Kai|tō do|men.   (Cliff 43Vc; Lamp 20)

Ashy head and dirty face.

How the Buddhas and Patriarchs look, blending in with this sordid world to set all beings free.

啐啄同時

105. Sot|taku dō|ji.   (Cliff 7Kc,16K)

Tap and peck at the same time.

The splendid achievement of master and student acting as one. When the egg's time has come, the chick taps with its beak on the inside of the eggshell, and at that same instant the mother hen pecks, breaking in from the outside.

団地一聲

106. Ka|ji is|sei.   (Spur)

"Ho!": One shout.

Great enlightenment's cry. For "Ho!" see #10. "Ji" stands for ":".

回光返照

107. E|kō hen|shō.   (Rinzai 1XX)

Turn that light inward—return, reflect.

Turn the light you've always had to look intently inward at who you yourself are!

坐久成勞

108. Za|kyū jin|rō.   (Cliff 17K)

Sitting long gets to be work.

A monk asked Kyōrin, "Why did the Patriarch [Bodhidharma] come from the West?" Kyōrin said, "Sitting long [as Bodhidharma did, facing a wall for nine years] gets to be work." Ahhh (a sigh of fatigue).

失錢遭罪

109. Shis|sen sō|zai.   (Cliff 8V)

Lose the cash *and* get the punishment.

Lose money, and then have to take the penalty for stealing it. An affair that's no longer profitable.

安心立命

110. An|jin ritsu|myō.   (Cliff 60Kn)

Mind at peace, set for life.

Body and mind at peace, a life based on wisdom is firmly settled. What's meant is that steady faith is established.

寒毛卓竪

111. Kam|mō taku|ju-su.   (Cliff 2Vn)

The fine hair on the skin stands erect.

The body hair [literally, "cold-hair"—insulation] bristling: Thrilling shock. '

賓主歷然

112. Hin|ju reki|nen.   (Rinzai 1IV)

Guest and host are obvious.

The difference between master and student is unmistakable. The distinction between guest and host is clear.

屙屎送尿

113. A|shi sō|nyō.   (Rinzai 1XII)

Taking shits, pissing, . . .

To defecate and urinate. These things are among those given [by Rinzai] as being everyone's everyday conduct [#162].

廓然無聖

114. Kaku|nen mu|shō.   (Cliff 1K)

Empty, not holy.

Like the sky clearing into solid color, one's mind and heart with not even a speck of cloudiness, a space wholly free of antagonistic dichotomies like vulgar/holy and have/be without. Complete, piercing, incomparable enlightenment's vista is meant.

拈華微笑

115. Nen|ge mi|shō.   (Mu 6K)

. . . held up a turning flower. There was a smile.

When the World-honored One turned a flower in his fingers, Kashō's face alone broke into a smile. This marks the direct transmission of silent insight, of "mind by mind".

指東劃西

116. Higashi-o$_x$ yubisa(shi nishi-o$_x$ kaku(su.   (Cliff 18Kn; Rinzai 1X)

Point East, indicating West.

Intentionally have it "Like this or like that?". Or, undecided whether it's one thing or another.

探竿影草

117. Tan|kan yō|zō.   (Cliff 10Kn; Rinzai 2XX)

A probing staff and shadowy form of grass.

Devices the master guides students with, sounding them out, listening to them. Probing staff: A pole for sounding (out); shadowy form of grass: A straw raincoat that cloaks the fisherman. These are also the tools he lures the fish with.

撥草參玄

118. Has|sō san|gen.   (Mu 47K)

Push the grasses aside to go deep.

Push the grasses aside: Make your way through tall weeds on a pilgrimage. Go deep: Thoroughly investigate the mysterious Buddhadharma. Make a pilgrimage in order to practice the Buddha's Way —and, clearing away the coarse underbrush of delusion, open the way to enlightenment.

擧一明三

119. Ko|ichi myō|san.   (Cliff 1I)

At the mention of one, clearly three.

Given one aspect, able to realize three more.

明明歷歷

120. Mei|mei reki|reki.

Bright, clear in every detail.

Vivid clarity Enlightenment's true body of reality vividly evident right before your eyes.

本來面目

121. Hon|rai-no mem|moku.   (Mu 23K)

The innate face-and-eye.

Your original true form, your self awakened to its own Buddha-nature, the real Self.   [Innate: Root, original, essential, fundamental.]

未在更道

122. Mi|zai sara-ni i(e.   (Equanimity 41K)

Not yet; say more!

That's still not OK; try speaking further.

東涌西沒

123. Tō|yu sai|botsu.   (Cliff 1I)

Rise in the East and go down in the West.

The idea is that of appearing and disappearing freely—and, the sun.

柳綠花紅

124. Yanagi-wa midori, hana-wa kurenai.

Willows are green, flowers red.

As you see it and as it is are both concrete aspects of the truth, manifestations of enlightenment.

枯木龍吟

125. Ko|boku ryū|gin.   (Kidō 2)

The dead tree's dragon hum.

The dragon hum is the sound of the wind against a dead tree. Taking the dead tree as death, inaction, and the dragon hum as energy, this is talking about life within death, movement within stillness.

歸家穩坐

126. Ki|ka on|za.   (Cliff 1Kc)

Return home: Sit calmly, solidly.

Returning to your own house after a long journey, you sit down tranquilly—and it's the same way with long-continued practice: At last you get to the "place" of insight, totally at peace!

死中得活

127. Shi|chū-ni katsu-o$_x$ e(tari.   (Cliff 4Vn)

Find life in death.

A miraculous turnaround: Turn from perfecting yourself to the practice of compassion for others.

棒頭有眼

128. Bō|tō-ni manako$_x$ a(ri.   (Cliff 75K)

On the stick's head there's an eye.

Never to hit blindly.

Calligraphy, phrase #8, by Eido Roshi

水中撈月

129.　Sui|chū-ni tsuki-o_x tora(u.

Fish for the moon in the water.

—a futile venture.

活潑潑地

130.　Kap|pap|pat|chi.　　(Cliff 98Vc; Rinzai 1XIV)

Vital, vital vitality!

Full of life, vigorous—free and to the point.

清風明月

131.　Sei|fū mei|getsu.　　(Zen 5)

Fresh wind, bright moon.

It's bracing to have not even a speck of delusion in the mind.

海晏河清

132.　Kai|an ka|sei.　　(Cliff 18Kc)

Sea calm, river clear.

The peace of nothing-doing in the heart's core. The weather fine, the voyage safe.

淵默雷轟

133.　Em|moku rai totoro(ku.　　(Cliff 84Kc)

The thunderclap of abyssal silence.

Like Vimalakīrti's thunderclap of silence [#26]. The abyss stands for deep integrity.

漆桶不會

134.　Shit|tsū fu|e.　　(Cliff 5K)

[As if in a] black lacquer pail, [you] don't understand.

Not understanding anything, as if in the darkness of a black lacquer pail.

滿面慚惶

135.　Mam|men-no zan|kō.　　(Cliff 2I)

The whole face confusedly attentive.

The face full of shame. Really disgraceful, to the limit.

18

烏龜鑽壁

136. U|ki kabe-o$_x$ ki(ru.   (Realm 1)

Blind turtle noses through the wall.

In blind ignorance, a turtle tries to break through a wall—a hopeless business.

無位眞人

137. Mu|i-no shin|nin.   (Rinzai, Preface and 1III)

Of no rank is the true man.

The man of true freedom, not at all subject to any rating—meaning, a man of complete, thorough enlightenment.

無依道人

138. Mu|e-no dō|nin.   (Rinzai 1XVI,XVII,XVIIIa,f)

Having no dependence: The man of the Way.

The independent, freestanding man of the Way, dependent on nothing whatsoever. One of complete, incomparable enlightenment.

熱喝嗔拳

139. Nek|katsu shin|ken.

A furious shout, a scolding fist.

The master, instead of grandmotherly kindness, sends forth a terrible thundering shout with a mighty clenched fist.

照顧脚下

140. Kya|ka-o$_x$ shō|ko-seyo..

Attentively watch your step.

Wherever you are going, be very careful of your steps. A monk asked, "Why did the Patriarch [Bodhidharma] come from the West?" The National Teacher Tōrei answered, "Attentively watch your step."

父子唱和

141. Fu|shi shō|wa-su.

Father and son chant in harmony.

When the father chants, the son chants in harmony. The mystery of father-and-son's family "style". The reference is to the Igyō sect's "house" tradition.

理事不二

142. Ri|ji fu|ni.   (Cliff 5I; Wreath)

Essence and event are not two.

Essence: The core of life—unconditioned, undifferentiated. Event: Appearances—relative, differentiated. Non-differentiation IS differentiation, differentiation IS non-differentiation, so essence and event are not separate things in opposition.

現成公案

143. Gen|jō kō|an.

The present event become the kōan.

Take the reality before your eyes NOW as your kōan. These facts before your eyes are the Buddha-nature's manifestations, its truth.

瓦解氷消

144. Ga|kai hyō|shō.   (Mu 19C)

The tile shatters, the ice melts.

A hundred years of doubt is settled one morning. It turns out to have been confusion.

目機銖兩

145. Mok|ki shu|ryō.   (Cliff 1I)

At a glance, catch the least difference.

Tell the difference of an exceedingly small [change in] weight [on a balance] with the naked eye—as an example of alert, shrewd and quick action.

眼横鼻直

146. Gan|nō bi|choku.

Eyes on the level, nose upright.

The directness of the Buddha-nature as it is. Your true character.

破家散宅

147. Ha|ka san|taku.   (Realm 7)

Wrecked house, scattered family.

Be ruined—meaning, escape all attachment of body and mind.

禍事禍事

148. Ka|ji ka|ji.   (Rinzai 1VI)

Deadly serious, deadly serious!

It's a serious matter, a serious matter. It's terrible, terrible!

和光同塵

149. Wa|kō dō|jin.　(Dào 4,56)

The mild light blends with the dust.

Concealing, not displaying, the glow of wit and intelligence, joining in with ordinary people, not asserting being "different," saving beings from suffering while involving ["blending"] oneself in worldly affairs ["dusts"], concealing one's own enlightened understanding.

和敬清寂

150. Wa|kei|sei|jaku.

Harmony, Reverence, Purity, Tranquillity.

Realizing the true meaning of the four characters of this phrase can begin with taking part in the Way of Tea. Harmony is the principle of unity, accord and peace. Reverence is the feeling of respect and affection for others. Purity is the principle of neat cleanliness—selfless, honest like a bright mirror. Tranquillity [Sanskrit, samādhi] is the principle of solitude—quiet—the wondrous state where ideas and thoughts are extinguished, even if only as an ideal.

空手還郷

151. Kū|shu-ni-shite kyō-ni$_x$ kae(ru.

Empty-handed, return home.

Empty-handed, empty of self, return to your true home. With nothing at all holding you, unconcernedly penetrate your own mental state.

紅旗閃爍

152. Kō|ki sen|shaku.

Red flags flashing.

Victory banners snapping in the sun. A criticism traditional in the Ummon sect.

綿綿密密

153. Mem|mem|mitsu|mitsu.

On and on in thick stillness.

Exact without the least break. [Careful practice.]

罵佛罵祖

154. Butsu-o$_x$ nonoshi(ri So-o$_x$ nonoshi(ru.　(Cliff 4K; Lamp 16)

Abuse the Buddha and curse the Patriarchs.

Acting according to Zen's First Principle, *everything* is swept away!

聖意難測

155. Shōi haka(ri $_x$ gata(shi.

The sages' intention is hard to fathom.

The compassion of the Buddhas and Patriarchs, being limitless, is beyond evaluation.

臥月眠雲

156. Tsuki-ni $_x$ fu(shi kumo-ni $_x$ nemu(ru.　(Kidō)

Lie in the moon, sleep in the clouds.

This is the state of the monk travelling with ease like moving clouds and flowing water.

著衣喫飯

157. Jaku|e kip|pan.　(Rinzai 1XII)

Dressing in clothes, eating meals.

—examples of everyday acts, all the things you do daily.

萬法一如

158. Bam|pō ichi|nyo.　(Faith 21:4; Rinzai 1XIII)

The myriad dharmas are one.

Every thing that is, is absolutely the same in its be-ing.

處處全眞

159. Sho|sho zen|shin.　(Cliff 36Vn)

At each place, the truth reveals itself completely.

Mountains and rivers, everything, are clear manifestations of the Dharma. The place you've arrived at is no other than the truth.

虛心坦懷

160. Kyo|shin tan|kai.

Detached mind, broad mind.

With no cares at all, vast calm.

衆流截斷

161. Shū|ru setsu|dan.　(Cliff 14Kc)

The myriad streamings cut off.

Completely break up delusion. "Myriad streamings" are the delusions of the passions and of ignorance.

行住坐臥

162. Gyō|jū|za|ga.　(Ummon 1)

Walking, standing, sitting, lying.

These "Four Dignities" stand for everything we do in everyday life.

言語道斷

163. Gon|go dō|dan.　(Faith 31:3)

The way of words cut off.

It can't be expressed in words—and statements are unnecessary.

説破了也

164. Sep|pa ryō|ya.

Spoke to destroy completely!

Confuted without a qualm.

陷虎之機

165. Kan|ko [no] ki.　(Cliff 79Kn)

A stratagem to entrap a tiger.

A trick to catch a tiger. Fierce actions of a stern Zen monk—mean that there's a fierce rebel within.

隔靴搔痒

166. Kutsu-o$_x$ heda(tete kayugari-o$_x$ ka(ku.　(Mu Preface)

Through the boot [he's] scratching the itch!

Doesn't serve the purpose at all. The effect contrary to what's intended.

隨波逐浪

167. Zui|ha chiku|rō.　(Cliff 14Kc)

Follow wave with wave.

Aptly respond to others in preaching the Dharma. Free, excelling action—the wondrous effect of differentiation.

隨處作主

168. Zui|sho-ni shu-to$_x$ na(ru.　(Rinzai 1XII)

Master going *with* situations.

Adapting to whatever environment without losing your freedom, be independent: Don't accept constraints from others.

鐵樹開花

169. Tetsu|ju hana-o$_x$ hira(ku.　(Cliff 40I)

The iron tree in bloom!

When all discriminative thinking is completely cut off, a great energy is newly born. The terse directness when understanding dawns.

露柱燈籠

170. Ro|chū tō|rō.　(Cliff 15Kc)

Revealed in pillar and lantern.

Before your eyes, both pillars and lanterns are concrete aspects of the wonderful truth of Buddhism.

露箇面目

171. Ko-no$_2$ mem|moku-o$_3$ ara(wasu$_1$.　(Cliff 16Kc)

Reveal one's own face.

The original face revealed as it actually is. Disclose and present the Self of enlightenment.

靈龜曳尾

172. Rei|ki o-o$_x$ hi(ku.　(Cliff 24I)

The marvelous tortoise drags its tail.

Trying to cover your traces, leave a trail behind in the process. The tortoise deposits its eggs in the sand and even covers them up, but then leaves a track behind dragging its tail.

非心非佛

173. Hi|shin hi|butsu.　(Mu 33K)

This very mind—NOT Buddha.

This phrase says "This very mind is the Buddha. [#103]" paradoxically. A monk asked, "What is the Buddha?" Baso said, "This very mind—NOT Buddha."

面壁九年

174. Mem|peki ku|nen.　(Cliff 1Kc)

Face the wall nine years.

Bodhidharma did zazen facing a wall for nine years at the Shǎo Lín Monastery on Mount Sōng in the state of Wèi.

頭上安頭

175. Zu|jō-ni zu-o$_x$ an(zu.　(Cliff 37Vn; Rinzai 1XVIIIc)

Puts a head atop his head.

A superfluous action—redundant, pointless.

24

體露金風

176. Tai|ro kim|pu.   (Cliff 27K)

Wholly revealed in the Golden Wind.

Wholly revealed: The whole is disclosed here and now. Golden Wind: The wind of autumn. The whole world full of the autumn wind's deep, soft rushing sound. A monk asked, "How is it when the trees perish (become bare) and the leaves fall?" Ummon replied, "Wholly revealed in the Golden Wind."

FIVE

一大事因緣

177. Ichi|dai|ji in|nen.   (Lotus 2)

The most important matter.

Shākyamuni's appearance in this world to bring all beings to realize the Buddha-mind. And, the Fundamental Principle of Zen: The Patriarchs' care to show generations beginning Zen practice the Way by example. And again, the practical discipline for realizing that Fundamental Principle.

一無位眞人

178. Ichi|mu|i-no shin|nin.   (Rinzai, Preface and 1III)

The one without rank, the true man.

This means the man who, whatever class he belongs to, is absolutely free—able to realize his true Self, his essential dignity, the Buddha-nature he has always had by nature.

一盲引衆盲

179. Ichi|mō shū|mō-o_x hi(ku.   (Cliff 5Kn; Mu 46V)

One of the blind leading on a multitude of the blind.

This is an exceedingly dangerous thing. A single bad teacher leads many students on an evil course.

八風吹不動

180. Hap|pū fu(kedomo dō(ze[zu.   (Zen 2)

Though the eight winds blow, it's unmoved.

The One Mind's calm stability is imperturbable. The "eight winds": Gain and loss, slander and honor, fame and ridicule, sorrow and joy—the eight kinds of things that agitate the human mind.

吾無隱乎爾

181. Ware nanji$_4$ [ni]$_3$ kaku(su-koto$_2$ na(shi$_1$.   (Analects)

I've nothing to hide from you.

Eagles hide nothing from you. The sphere of enlightenment is plain to see before your eyes.

壺中日月長

182. Ko|chū jitsu|getsu naga(shi.

The pot: Within, sun and moon are constant.

In another world (that of enlightenment), time doesn't exist. According to legend, during the Later Han a hermit called the Lord of the Pot made a pot his dwelling.

大道透長安

183. Dai|dō Chō|an-ni$_x$ tō(ru.   (Zen 5)

The Great Way goes to Cháng-ān.

The true Great Way passes into the capital [Buddha's abode]. Cháng-ān was the [ancient Chinese] capital.

好事不如無

184. Kō|zu-mo na(ki-ni-wa$_x$ shi(ka[zu.   (Cliff 86K)

A good thing is nothing like no thing.

However wonderful it may be to do something, it may well be that it would be better not to have done it after all. Nothing-doing is exactly what's most valuable. Even enlightenment can't compare with having broken your attachments.

山深雪未消

185. Yama fuka(u-shite yuki ima(da ki(ezu.   (Kidō 2)

The snow deep in the mountains hasn't yet melted away.

In mountain recesses spring is late and some snow still remains. The actual state of attainment now.

山色清淨身

186. San|shoku shō|jō|shin.

The mountains' form is clear: A pure body.

A fine mountain landscape is, as it is, the fine, honorable form of the Buddha.

平常心是道

187. Byō|jō|shin ko(re dō.   (Mu 19K)

The ordinary mind is the Way.

The mind as it is that takes every day as it comes is the Dào [Way]. Jōshū asked Nansen, "What is the Way?" Nansen said, "The ordinary mind is the Way."

26

庭前柏樹子

188. Tei|zen-no haku|ju|shi.   (Mu 37K)

The cypress tree in the garden[: Before this room].

With a single cypress tree standing in the garden right before his eyes, the monk asked Jōshū, "Why did Bodhidharma come from the West?" Jōshū said, "The cypress tree in the garden," referring to "The meaning of the Patriarch's coming from the West." [#206.]

慈眼視衆生

189. Ji|gen shu|jō-o $_x$ mi(ru.   (Lotus 25)

Compassion's eye watches over all beings.

Buddhas and bodhisattvas are able to look with pity on all beings with their eye of compassion.

擔雪填古井

190. Yuki-o $_x$ nina(tte ko|sei-o $_x$ uzu(mu.   (Ranks 5)

Carrying snow, they fill the old well.

Bringing snow, they fill the well—and can't fill it up. It's useless work, with no result. This speaks of the life of limitless great compassion—ashy head, dirty face, saving all beings from suffering, never giving up—said of one of great enlightenment.

日出乾坤輝

191. Hi i(dete ken|kon kagaya(ku.   (Zen 2)

The sun comes out; the heavens and the earth are alight.

The uncaused, spontaneously self-existent aspect of things. The heavens and the earth: The whole universe!

日日是好日

192. Nichi|nichi ko(re kō|jitsu.   (Cliff 6K)

Every day is a good day.

Wholeheartedly nothing-doing, what do you have to worry about? It's enough to rejoice in the sublime fact of this day right now.

時時勤拂拭

193. Ji ji-ni tsuto(mete fus|shiki-se-yo.   (Platform 6)

Ever and again diligently wipe it clean.

Continually working, wipe away the dusts of the mind. Jinshū [Shén-xiù] said in verse: "The body is the Bodhi [Enlightenment] tree/ The mind like a bright mirror's stand./ Ever and again diligently wipe it clean/ For it must not collect dust."

更參三十年

194. Sara-ni san(zeyo san|jū|nen.   (Cliff 20V2n)

Reflect further—thirty years more.

Gaining a little headway, you must not be satisfied. In the practice pride must be avoided. Now you must practice more and more.

曹源一滴水

195. Sō|gen-no it|teki|sui.   (Cliff 7Kc)

The Cáo Wellspring's one drop of water.

The Cáo Wellspring is Sōkei, [where] the Sixth Patriarch Enō [lived and taught]. He, being a wellspring of the Dharma, let out one drop of the correct doctrine—meaning, the root spirit of Zen.

本來無一物

196. Hon|rai mu|ichi|motsu.   (Platform 8)

Fundamentally not a thing exists.

The root is where I'm coming from, saying there is not even a single thing. These words are a direct presentation of Zen experience. The point of this teaching is that while all existence is the occurrence of phenomena based on causation [karma], that is not the case with your root self-nature. [See #193 and #629.]

松樹千年翠

197. Shō|ju sen|nen-no midori.

The pine-trees' thousand-year blue.

Happiness praising the millenial slightly purplish blue-green of the towering old pines.

東山水上行

198. Tō|zan sui|jō kō.   (Realm 4)

The eastern mountain walks on the water.

The mountain to the east walks on the water's surface. Freedom of action after enlightenment. A monk asked Ummon, "Where is it that all the Buddhas are from?" Ummon said, "The eastern mountain walks on the water."

步步是道場

199. Ho|bo ko(re dō|jō.

Each step is the training place.

Every place you go is right in the midst of enlightenment. Neither standing nor sitting will make you enlightened.

步步清風起

200. Ho|bo sei|fū oko(ru.   (Realm 4)

At each step cool breeze rises.

When the mind gets free of rubbish, the place it gets to is refreshing. The mental state of one ready to attain enlightenment.

無事是貴人

201. Bu|ji ko(re ki|nin.   (Rinzai 1XI)

Nothing-doing: The valuable man.

I call one gone beyond perplexity and understanding, one with the will to depend on nothing, the really valuable man.

獨坐大雄峰

202. Doku|za Dai|yū|hō.   (Cliff 26K)

Alone I sit on Great Courage Peak.

Sitting down solidly, alone on Great Courage Peak. A sublime environment of isolated freedom. Daiyū Peak is another name for Hyakujō Mountain. A monk asked Hyakujō, "What is the miracle here?" Hyakujō said, "Alone I sit on Daiyū Peak."

白雲抱幽石

203. Haku|un yū|seki-o$_x$ ida(ku.   (Hán-shān)

White clouds enfold dark rocks.

A mysterious scene in the mountain recesses. The quiet place in the heart of the man of the Way.

直心是道場

204. Jiki|shin ko(re dō|jō.   (Vimalakīrti)

The straightforward mind is the training place.

When the mind gets free of discrimination and delusion, that moment in that place is the cleared training ground wherein one is ready for enlightenment.

眼前是什麼

205. Gan|zen ko(re na|n-zo.

Right before your eyes is—what?

This something is arrayed before your eyes! The phrase is suggesting something more than shapes.

祖師西來意

206. So|shi sei|rai|i. (Cliff 17K)

Why the Patriarch came out of the West.

The meaning and intention of Bodhidharma's coming from India in the West to China. Buddhism's core meaning, Zen's true marrow.

神光照天地

207. Shin|kō ten|chi-o$_x$ te(rasu. (Cliff 96V1)

The spiritual light illumines heaven and earth.

The light of Mind, the bright future of real intention, shines brightly over the whole universe.

荒草鋤不盡

208. Kō|sō su(ki tsu(kusa[zu.

With wild grasses, the weeding is never done.

No matter how much you dig, you don't run out of weeds to spade up. You don't run out of delusions to clear away either.

萬里無片雲

209. Ban|ri hen|un$_x$ na(shi. (Zen 6)

For ten thousand miles, not a wisp of cloud.

The sun bright in a clear sky. The state of mind of great enlightenment.

通身是手眼

210. Tsū|shin ko(re shu|gen. (Cliff 89K)

Throughout, the body is hand and eye.

The whole body is hand and eye. The thousand-handed Kannon's immeasurable, limitless, surpassing action.

通身無影像

211. Tsū|shin yō|zō$_x$ na(shi. (Cliff 90Kn)

Throughout the body, not the shadow of a form.

The universe and this one body are not two. The body alight through and through.

金剛王寶劍

212. Kon|gō|ō|hō|ken. (Rinzai 2XX)

The Diamond King's jeweled sword.

The sword of victory that cuts off all distress and delusion for good. In the *Rinzai Roku:* "Sometimes a single Gkhaught!—is like the Diamond King's jeweled sword."

銀宛裏盛雪

213. Gin|wan|ri-ni yuki-o$_x$ mo(ru.   (Cliff 13K; Mirror 5; Realm 5:7K)

The silver bowl is filled with snow.

Fill near-white with white—similar and dissimilar: Limitless splendor.

雲消山嶽露

214. Kumo ki(ete san|gaku ara(waru.   (Compendium)

The clouds melt away and the mountain peaks are revealed.

The invigorating blue mountains are beautiful against the sky, a splendid panorama. The wonder of events like the amazing present one.

面南見北斗

215. Minami-ni $_x$ mukat(te hoku|to-o$_x$ mi(ru.   (Cliff 28V)

Facing south, see the Big Dipper.

Freedom of action after enlightenment—or it can signify impossibility.

鰕跳予出斗

216. Ka odo(re-domo, to-o$_x$ i(de[zu.   (Cliff 6Kn)

The shrimp jumps about, but can't escape the measure.

No matter how much the little shrimp leaps about, he can't get out of the square measuring box. No matter how much noise one without ability makes, it's no great affair. And there's no way to escape but enlightenment.

SIX

一花開天下春

217. Ik|ka hira(ite ten|ka haru-nari.

A single flower blooms and it's spring under heaven.

With a single blossom, spring comes round, covering the ground.

上是天下是地

218. Kami-wa ko(re ten, shimo-wa ko(re chi.   (Cliff 6Vn)

The sky's above, the ground's below.

The *incomparable* self-existent underlying reality.

不思善不思惡

219. Fu|shi|zen fu|shi|aku.　(Mu 23K; Platform 11)

Don't think "good," don't think "evil".

This points toward a place wholly above and beyond the dichotomies of good/evil and right/wrong. Words of Enō [Huì Néng], the Sixth Patriarch.

也太奇也太奇

220. Ya|tai|ki ya|tai|ki.

Terrific! Terrific!

Oh, how wonderful! A shout of pleasant surprise.

井覷驢驢覷井

221. I ro-o$_x$mi, ro i-o$_x$mi(ru.　(Zen 2)

The well watches the ass, the ass watches the well.

The splendid ability of no-mind and no-mind to be reflected in each other.

入虎穴捋虎鬚

222. Ko|ketsu-ni$_x$ i(tte ko|shu-o$_x$na(zu.　(Rinzai Preface, 3I; Zen 9)

Go into the tiger's cave and pull the tiger's whiskers.

Ready to lose his life without so much as looking back.

兩箇無孔鐵鎚

223. Ryō|ko mu|ku-no tet|tsui.　(Realm 6:3Kn; Zen 16)

Two perfect—each with no hole—iron hammers.

Two men alike remarkable. And, the real (everywhere the same) and the customary (discrimination of differences) pounded into a unity.

前三三後三三

224. Zen|san|san go|san|san.　(Cliff 35K)

To the front threes, threes, and behind threes, threes.

Before you and in back, anywhere you look and right over there, all full. Uncountable, infinite.

半河南半河北

225. Nakaba-wa ka|nan, nakaba-wa ka|hoku.　(Cliff 6Kn, 83Kn)

Half on the river's south side, half to the river's north.

It's not stated whether it's north of the river or south of the river.

南山雲北山雨

226.　Nan|zan-wa kumo, hoku|zan-wa ame.

The south mountains cloudy, the north mountains rainy.

The marvel of nature's spontaneity. And, an aspect of the nature of the truth.

古佛與露柱交

227.　Ko|butsu [to] ro|chū-to maji(waru.　(Cliff 83K; Realm 5:19)

The old Buddha communes with the exposed pillar.

The old Buddha and the central pillar (symbol of the Wealth Deity) make a vow to associate on intimate terms. The freedom of action after enlightenment.

吾道一以貫之

228.　Wa(ga michi, itsu mot(te kore-o$_x$ tsuranu(ku.　(Analects)

My Way: Penetrating THIS with the One.

The great Way beyond compare, penetrating the whole universe and all ages.

嗔拳不打笑面

229.　Shin|ken shō|men-o$_x$ ta(se[zu.　(Realm 6:1Vc)

An angry fist won't strike a smiling face.

Even a fist clenched in wrath won't hit a smiling countenance. It says just this: What no hand at all could touch.

天下人不知價

230.　Ten|ka-no hito atai-o$_x$ shi(ra[zu.　(Cliff 8V)

No one under heaven knows what it's worth.

Nobody knows the true value of enlightenment.

天是天地是地

231.　Ten-wa ko(re ten, chi-wa ko(re chi.　(Arsenal)

The sky's the sky, the ground's the ground.

Reality as you find it is its true aspect. A subtle aspect of enlightenment as it is.

山是山水是水

232.　Yama-wa ko(re yama, mizu-wa ko(re mizu.

Mountains are mountains, rivers are rivers.

Reality as you find it is its true aspect. A subtle aspect of enlightenment as it is.

急水上打毬子

233. Kyū|sui|jō-ni kyū|su-o_x ta(su.   (Cliff 80K)

A ball dashed onto rapids.

Even a moment of carelessness and the ball darts away for good. Without an unguarded moment for so much as a hair of discrimination to get in.

懸羊頭賣狗肉

234. Yō|tō-o_x kaka(gete ku|niku-o_x u(ru.   (Mu 6C)

Hang out a sheep's head and sell dog meat.

The things on sale are a sham—aren't what's on the signboard. Between mouth [speech] and belly [intention] there is a great difference.

日面佛月面佛

235. Nichi|men|butsu, gachi|men|butsu.   (Cliff 3K,V)

Sun-faced Buddha, Moon-faced Buddha.

It's unnecessary to go into "sun-faced" and "moon-faced"—just see that the earnestness of the Zen Master Baso is in this phrase! When Baso was ill, the head monk asked, "How is your reverence doing these days?" Great Master Baso said, "Sun-faced Buddha, Moon-faced Buddha."

明歷歷露堂堂

236. Mei|reki|reki, ro|dō|dō.

Clear in detail, revealed in splendor!

Naked clarity with not even a speck hidden. Revealed: Apparent.

明皎皎白的的

237. Mei|kō|kō, haku|teki|teki.

Clear glistening white, bright and clear in detail.

The idea is exceeding clarity. Glistening white: Moonlight round about.

昨日雨今日晴

238. Saku|jitsu-wa ame, kon|nichi-wa hare.

Yesterday, rain—today, clear.

The truth manifest, reality as it is. The wonder of enlightenment as you find it.

朝三千暮八百

239. Chō|san|zen, bo|hap|pyaku.   (Cliff 66Vn)

Mornings three thousand, evenings eight hundred.

Three thousand blows in the morning, eight hundred blows in the evening. Beating, beating, beating until you fall forward.

李花白桃花紅

240. Ri|ka-wa shiro(ku tō|ka-wa kurenai-nari.

Plum blossoms are white, peach blossoms red.

The visible revelation of the entire body of Truth and Law. The same as "Willows green, flowers red."

柳下綠花下紅

241. Yanagi midori-nara[zu hana kurenai-nara[zu.

Willows are not green, flowers not red.

The body of Truth and Law as the body at hand. The true face beyond compare, everywhere the same.

湘之南潭之北

242. Shō [no] minnami, Tan [no] kita.　(Cliff 18K)

South of the River Xiāng and north of the Tán River.

Meaning, a locality you go hither and thither in. (The point doesn't necessarily have to do with a particular district.)

殺人刀活人劍

243. Satsu|jin|tō, katsu|jin|ken.　(Mu 11V)

The sword that kills a man is the sword that brings him to life.

The power of life and death is having the sword of enlightenment in your hand.

江月照松風吹

244. Kō|getsu te(rashite shō|fū fu(ku.　(Song 24:5)

The river moon shines, the pine wind blows.

Surroundings subtly wonderful under the stamp of enlightenment. The deep place where even the foul odor of enlightenment is gone. The breath-melting incomparable underlying reality.

無孔笛最難吹

245. Mu|ku|teki motto(mo fu(ki$_x$ gata(shi.　(Comprehensive)

The flute with no holes is the hardest to blow.

You can't blow a flute with no holes. In enlightenment's directness, means are suddenly on hand.

父不嚴子不孝

246. Chichi gen-nara[zare(ba ko kō-nara[zu.　(Kidō 2)

The father not strict, the son not respectful.

A child not brought up and taught with strictness becomes disobedient to its parents.

牛頭沒馬頭回

247. Go|zu bos(shi me|zu kae(ru.   (Cliff 5V)

The ox-head vanishes; the horsehead returns.

A metaphor for incessant birth-and-death and ups-and-downs—and elusiveness. It has nothing to do with ox and horse.

痴兀兀兀兀痴

248. Chi|kotsu|kotsu, kotsu|kotsu|chi.   (Comprehensive 29)

Idiotically steadfast: A steadfast idiot.

Detachment, becoming a fool from head to foot. Steadfast: The state of unknowing.

禍不入慎家門

249. Wazawai-wa shin|ka-no$_2$ mon-ni$_3$ i(ra[zu$_1$.   (Comprehensive 13)

Calamities never enter the careful household's door.

Where self-control is not forgotten, disasters don't come to pass.

空手來空手去

250. Kū|shu-ni-shite kita(ri kū|shu-ni-shite sa(ru.   (Kidō 4)

Empty-handed he comes, empty-handed he goes.

Indicates the lot of the excellent Zen monk—without illusion, without attachment, without a single thing.

胡長三黑李四

251. Ko|Chō|san koku|Ri|shi.   (Arsenal)

The bearded Zhāng sons are three in number; the swarthy Lǐ sons, four.

The tendency of dialects to lump people together in speaking of them. Zhāng and Lǐ are Chinese family names. The point is the extent to which they're called the bearded three sons and the swarthy four sons.

草茸茸煙羃羃

252. Kusa|jō|jō kemuri|beki|beki.   (Cliff 6V)

Grass shoots beyond shoots, mist layer on layer.

"Shoots beyond shoots" are grasses growing rampant; "layer on layer" is mist rising thickly all around. Exquisite reality, as it is.

藏頭白海頭黑

253. Zō|tō haku, Kai|tō koku.   (Cliff 73K,V)

Zō's head is white; Kai's head is black.

Chizō's head is white; the head of [another disciple of Baso—Hyakujō] Ekai—is black. If that fellow is that fellow, this fellow is this fellow. The idea is that they are equally adept.

36

行亦禪坐亦禪

254. Gyō-mo mata Zen, za-mo mata Zen.　(Song 20)

Walking is also Zen, sitting is also Zen.

Zen is not sitting looking one way; walking, standing, sitting and lying down are all Zen. "Coming and going won't take you other places/Singing and dancing are the voice of the Dharma." [—Hakuin's "Song of Zazen," lines 35 and 37—in DS.]

踞地金毛獅子

255. Ko|ji kim|mō-no shi|shi.　(Rinzai 2XX)

Crouching on the ground: The golden-haired lion.

The lion, with gold fur, crouching down on the ground, stalks his prey. Said of a master whose great strength and magnanimity conceal a sharp point within.

金烏急玉兎速

256. Kin|u kyū-ni gyoku|to sumi(yaka-nari.　(Cliff 12V)

The gold-sheen crow is quick; the jade-white hare is swift.

In enlightenment's excelling movement, discrimination is hard to get in—the circumstances change so swiftly. The gold-sheen crow is the sun; the jade-white hare, the moon.

鉢裏飯桶裏水

257. Hatsu|ri|han, tsū|ri|sui.　(Cliff 50K)

Rice in the bowl, water in the pail.

In the bowl is rice; in the pail is water. The splendor of individual things one by one.

鎮州出大蘿蔔

258. Chin|jū-ni dai|ra|fu-o$_x$ ida(su.　(Cliff 30K)

Chinshū produces huge radishes.

Radishes are a specialty of Chinshū (the district where Jōshū, the master saying these words, lived). That way.

鐵牛通身無骨

259. Tetsu|gyū tsū|shin hone$_x$ na(shi.

The iron ox is, throughout his body, without bones.

The iron ox is entirely of iron alone, without impurities.

龜毛長兔角短

260. Ki|mō-wa naga(ku, to|kaku-wa mijika(shi.

The turtle's hair is long, the hare's horns short.

Freedom of action after enlightenment. There is no such thing as hair on the turtle and horns on the rabbit.

SEVEN

一句講了一切經

261. Ik|ku-ni is|sai|kyō-o$_x$ kō|ryō(su.

One word makes all the sutras clear, once and for all.

This refers to the splendid activity that settles the universe in a phrase and subdues the world at a stroke.

一喝如雷聞者喪

262. Ik|katsu rai-no$_x$ goto(ku ki(ku mono sō(su.

One thundering GKHAUGHT!—and he who hears dies.

Everyone within earshot of the shout like a thunderclap loses his life.

一心只在梅花上

263. Is|shin-wa tada bai|ka-no$_2$ ue-ni$_3$ a(ri$_1$.   (Jōwa 9)

The One Mind just being on the plum blossom.

Admiring the flowering plum is plum samādhi.

一曲琵琶奏月明

264. Ik|kyoku-no bi|wa getsu|mei-ni$_x$ sō(su.

A tune the lute plays to the moonlight.

Beautiful sounds in the moonlight. Infinite refinement.

一段風光畫不成

265. Ichi|dan-no fū|kō ega-kedomo na(ra[zu.   (Comprehensive 28)

However much a landscape is painted at, it's still incomplete

The natural beauty of this mind's vista can't be expressed in pictures or poems.

一聲幽鳥到窓前

266. Is|sei-no yū|chō sō|zen-ni$_x$ ita(ru.   (Chūhō)

With just one call the mountain bird comes before the window.

The charm of a mountain hut. A finely subtle aspect of reality as it actually is.

38

一聲雷震清風起

267. Is|sei rai furu(tte sei|fū oko(ru.   (Cliff 49V)

With a single thunderclap's shock pure breeze rises.

A splendid, refreshing circumstance. An image for the frame of mind of Great Enlightenment.

一聲霹靂驚天地

268. Is|sei-no heki|reki ten|chi-o$_x$ odoro(kasu.   (Jōwa 8)

A single thunderclap: Crack!—shocks the heavens and the earth.

A metaphor for the clear-eyed master's one word, one phrase.

一聲鷄唱乾坤曉

269. Is|sei tori-wa tona(u ken|kon-no akatsuki.   (Jōwa 9)

With one crow the cock heralds the universal dawn.

An unchanging universal principle: With one sound the darkness is gone.

一葉落知天下秋

270. Ichi|yō o(chite ten|ka-no$_2$ aki-o$_3$ shi(ru$_1$.

By one leaf's fall know it's autumn under heaven.

The coming of fall with a single leaf of the paulownia tree. And this is the way enlightenment happens.

一超直入如來地

271. Ic|chō jiki|nyū Nyo|rai|ji.   (Song 23:8)

One leap right into the Tathāgata state.

Sudden Bodhi (Enlightenment), without going through stages.

一雨普潤周沙界

272. Ichi|u amane(ku uruo(shite sha|kai-ni$_x$ amane(shi.

The one rain everywhere imbues the worlds all around,
  Many as the sands of the Ganges.

The rain of the Buddha-dharma's compassion waters—quickens—the great universe of worlds numerous as the Ganges' sand grains.

一鳥不鳴山更幽

273. Ic|chō na(ka[zu yama sara-ni yū-nari.

The lone bird makes no cry; mountains are yet more mysterious.

One's condition deep in the mountains, hushed, secluded, free of conventions. And this is enlightenment's frame of mind.

三人行必有我師

274. San|nin yu(ku-toki-wa kanara(zu waga|shi$_x$a(ri.　(Analects 7XXI)

Of three men in succession, one is invariably my master.

When three people meet together, one of them turns out to be the one who excels.

三千里外有知音

275. San|zen|ri|gai chi|in$_x$a(ri.　(Jōwa 8)

Three thousand miles away you've an intimate friend.

An intimate comrade seems to converse with you, even at a distance.

三千里外沒交涉

276. San|zen|ri|gai mok|kyō|shō.　(Cliff 83Kn)

Three thousand miles away: Out of touch.

Meaning, so distant there's no approaching him.

三更杲日黑漫漫

277. San|kō-no kō|jitsu koku|mam|man.　(Eye 2)

In the third watch the bright sun is vastly, fully dark.

The great sun is jet black all night. In a cave, even if the sun is at its brightest, no one can see. [The third watch is 11 PM – 1 AM.]

上下四維無等匹

278. Jō|ge shi|yui tō|hitsu$_x$na(shi.　(Cliff 6V)

Up, down and in the four directions, you've no equal.

No one under heaven is comparable. The state of the Alone-honored One [the Buddha]. The "four directions" are the NE, SE, SW and NW quarters.

不動一步行千里

279. Ip|po-o$_x$dō(ze[zu-shite sen|ri-o$_x$yu(ku.

Without moving one step, go a thousand miles.

Not moving your feet at all, go a thousand miles. Unselfconscious excellence of action, enlightenment's supple dynamism.

不斷煩惱入涅槃

280. Bon|nō-o$_x$dan(ze[zu-shite ne|han-ni$_x$i(ru.　(Hymn 6)

Without cutting off pain and distress, go into nirvāṇa.

Nirvāṇa is the state of enlightenment. True enlightenment is to realize completely, *with* pain and distress [delusion]. (The original reads, ". . . *attain* nirvāṇa.")

不知明月落誰家

281. Shi(ra[zu mei|getsu ta-ga₂ ie-ni-ka₃ o(tsu₁.

There's no telling whose house the bright moonlight will fall into.

Compassion having unstinted admiration for the bright moon.

不離魔界入佛界

282. Ma|kai-oₓ hana(re[zu-shite Buk|kai-niₓ i(ru.

Not leaving Māra's realm, enter Buddha's realm.

The Zen monk's true sphere of action is deliberate, free use of the dual world of Buddha-Māra [enlightenment/delusion].

丙丁童子來求火

283. Hei|tei|dō|ji rai gu ka.

Heiteidōji comes looking for fire.

Heiteidōji is the god of fire. The fire god in search of fire. The idea is that while each of us has his own Buddha-nature, we seek the Buddha-nature in others.

也勝秋露滴芙渠

284. Mata shū|ro-no₂ fu|kyo-ni₄ shitata(ru-ni₃ masa(reri₁.   (Cliff 36K)

Still more excellent—the autumn dewdrops on lotus petal furrows.

A scene like no other—refreshing and pure.

兩刃交鋒不須避

285. Ryō|jin hokosaki-oₓ maji(ete sa(kuru-koto-oₓ mochi(i[zu.   (Ranks 4)

Two swords cross points: No need to dodge.

Neither hands thrust forward nor hands drawn back. The mysterious give-and-take of two mirrors reflecting each other's light. [This is followed by #299.]

前箭猶輕後箭深

286. Zen|sen-wa nao karu(ku kō|sen-wa fuka(shi.   (Cliff 93V)

The first arrow was light; the second struck deep.

The first remark is not so crushing, but the second is scathing.

十字街頭破草鞋

287. Jū|ji|gai|tō-no ha|sō|ai.

A torn-apart straw sandal where the street enters the intersection.

Throwing it away, turning from everyone (oneself included), be perverse.

千聖從來不識伊

288. Sen|shō jū|rai kare-o$_x$ shi(ra[zu.

The thousands of sages up till now haven't understood Him.

You couldn't say that even the likes of Shākyamuni and Bodhidharma understood the directness of enlightenment.

千里萬里一條鐵

289. Sen|ri ban|ri ichi|jō-no tetsu.

For a thousand miles, ten thousand miles, a straight line hard as iron.

Only the Buddha-nature exists, piercing through the solid earth and the whole universe.

南山打皷北山舞

290. Nan|zan-ni tsuzumi-o$_x$ u(teba hoku|san-ni ma(u.   (Ummon)

South mountain beats the drum while north mountain dances.

The action of the freedom that goes beyond dichotomous distinctions. With enlightenment there is no far and near.

同死同生爲君訣

291. Dō|shi dō|shō kimi-ga$_x$ tame-ni kes(su.   (Cliff 15V)

He goes through the same death and the same birth with you,
  And you part.

To go with and chime in with each other. Intimate, at bottom kindred souls, wholeheartedly of a mind, experience as one.

坐斷天下人舌頭

292. Ten|ka-no$_2$ hito-no$_3$ zet|tō-o$_4$ za|dan-su$_1$.   (Cliff 13I)

Cut out the tongues of everyone under heaven.

Marvelous activity no one in the world can talk about, even with great effort.

大唐打皷新羅舞

293. Dai Tō-ni tsuzumi-o$_x$ u(teba Shin|ra-ni ma(u.   (Cliff 24Kn)

They're beating the drum in Great Táng as they dance in Silla.

Striking the drum with no mind to do so, dancing with no mind to do so. [Great Táng: China; Silla: Korea.]

大地山河絶纖埃

294. Dai|ji sen|ga sen|ai-o$_x$ zes(su.

In the wide world, the mountains and rivers,
  Not even the finest dust particle.

The condition of the enlightened state of mind, not even the suggestion of a cloud [of ignorance] hanging in the mind.

42

大地撮來無寸土

295. Daiji sas(shi kita(ru-ni sun|do$_x$ na(shi.　(Eye 1)

From the vast earth, pinch up—not even an inch of land.

Pinch up soil of the great earth, not even a lick. The light and open air of great enlightenment, the vista beyond discrimination of whether the area is great or small.

大鵬一擧九萬里

296. Tai|hō ik|kyo-su kyū|man|ri.

An enormous bird whose every move takes ninety thousand miles.

The fabulous rukh covers 90,000 miles in flapping its wings. The excellent Zen monk's tremendous actions.

大鵬展翅取龍吞

297. Tai|hō shi-o$_x$ no(bete ryū-o$_x$ to(tte no(mu.　(Chūhō)

The giant rukh spreads its wings to catch a dragon and then devours it.

The giant rukh is the golden-winged garuḍa, a great bird that lives on dragons, its magnificent resources overwhelming.

天下衲僧跳不出

298. Ten|ka-no nō|sō chō|fu|shutsu.　(Cliff 33V)

All the robed monks under heaven jump about and can't escape.

No one, no matter who, can get out of the sphere of enlightenment.

好手還同火裏蓮

299. Kō|shu kae(tte ka|ri-no$_2$ ren-ni$_3$ ona(ji$_1$.　(Ranks 4)

The master swordsman is the same as a lotus in fire.

One who has completely mastered his discipline is unscathed by fire and flood.

子規啼落西山月

300. Shi|ki na(ki oto(su sei|zan-no tsuki.　(Comprehensive 16)

The cuckoo calls the setting of the moon into the western hills.

The light, airy feeling of the cuckoo's call under the moon at dawn—a state of mind and heart.

張公喫酒李公醉

301. Chō|kō sake-o$_x$ kis(sureba Ri|kō yo(u.　(Ummon)

When Mr. Zhāng drinks wine Mr. Lǐ gets drunk.

The freedom of action after enlightenment, above and beyond discrimination between oneself and others. Zhāng and Lǐ are (any) common family names.

德不孤兮必有隣

302. Toku-wa ko-nara[zu — kanarazu tonari_x a(ri.   (Analects 4XXV)

Virtue is not lone!—there are sure to be neighbors.

People invariably draw near where virtue shines.

抛却黄金拾瓦礫

303. Ō|gon-o_x hō|kyaku-shite ga|reki-o_x hiro(u.   (Lamp 17)

Throw away yellow gold and pick up pottery fragments.

The bodhisattva vows and undergoes the discipline, not stopping in enlightenment's exaltation, to emancipate all beings in the workaday world below from suffering.

拈來瓦礫是黄金

304. Nen(ji kita(reba ga|reki-mo ko(re ō|gon.

Pick out ceramic shards and they're gold coins.

Picked up one by one, even debris is none other than the glory of the Buddha.

擾擾忽忽水裏月

305. Jō|jō sō|sō sui|ri-no tsuki.   (Cliff 15V)

The moon in the agitated, restless water.

The moon in the water, fragmented a million-fold, isn't swept away. The wonderful state of mind of both clarity and darkness (adapted to each other as action and inaction, discrimination and non-discrimination, are). Agitated: Confused, disturbed; restless: Rushed, busy—all of which the water's movement represents.

新婦騎驢阿家牽

306. Shim|pu ro-ni_x no(reba a|ko hi(ku.   (Equanimity 65)

The bride rides an ass her mother-in-law leads.

The state of mind of no-mind. This event's marvelous aspect.

日出東方夜落西

307. Hi-wa tō|hō-yori_x i(dete yoru nishi-ni_x o(tsu.   (Eye 2)

The sun comes out of the East and in the evening sets in the West.

That way. The marvel of awakening to reality as you find it.

明月蘆花君自看

308. Mei|getsu ro|ka kimi mizuka(ra mi(yo.   (Cliff 62V)

The moonlight on the reed flowers you see on your own!

You see this scene in your own mind! The ebb and flow of your own enlightenment, your self-understanding.

44

明眼衲僧會不得

309. Mei|gen-no nō|sō-mo e|fu|toku.　(Cliff 73V)

Even clear-eyed robed monks are unable to understand this.

You couldn't say that even the Buddhas and Patriarchs understand the clear directness of enlightenment.

昨夜三更月到窓

310. Saku|ya san|kō tsuki mado-ni$_x$ ita(ru.　(Kidō 1)

Last night in the third watch the moon reached the window.

The excellent circumstance of being-and-becoming as you find it. The exquisite state of the mind free of illusion. [The third watch is 11 PM – 1 AM.]

月在青天水在瓶

311. Tsuki-wa sei|ten-ni$_x$ a(ri mizu-wa hei-ni$_x$ a(ri.　(Realm 4)

The moon's in the blue sky, water's in the bottle.

Straight ahead that way. Enlightenment's subtle taste.

朝聞道夕死可也

312. Ashita-ni michi-o$_x$ ki(keba yūbe-ni shi(su-tomo ka nari.　(Analects 4VIII)

If in the morning one follows the Way
　In the evening he dies content.

These words strongly express the importance of peace of mind, of certainty (the Great Way's realization). And again, they reveal the splendor of this peace of mind and certainty.

杜鵑啼處花狼藉

313. To|ken na(ku tokoro hana rō|zeki.　(Kidō 2)

Flowers grow in profusion where the cuckoo calls.

The sentence as it stands. Reality, as it is, is the wonder of enlightenment.

枯木花開劫外春

314. Ko|boku hana hira(ku gō|gai-no haru.　(Eye 1)

The decayed tree's flowers open in the timeless spring.

The supreme action: Without regrets, without purposes. The manifestation of the independence that clears away dichotomies, having risen above them. The spring landscape reflected in the mind's eye of profound enlightenment. "The timeless spring" is the spring that transcends history and time.

柏樹子話有賊機

315. Haku|ju|shi-no wa-ni zok|ki$_x$ a(re.

In the kōan about the oak there is a thief's stratagem.

This means that there is a thief's move in Jōshū Zenji's "The oak [more literally, cypress or cedar] in the garden." (Mu 37K) "Thief's stratagem" is a term of Kanzan Kokushi—referring to the terrific action that suddenly snatches away everything.

相識猶如不相識

316. Sō|shiki-wa nao fu|sō|shiki-no goto(shi.   (Realm 5)

To know each other is just like not to know each other.

Since intimate friends know each other's hearts thoroughly, each seems like yet another person. ["Know"—discriminatively.]

栴檀葉葉香風起

317. Sen|dan yō|yō kō|fū oko(ru.

From the spreading chinaberry's many leaves fragrant breezes come.

The chinaberry is an aromatic tree. The leaves waving, the soughing wind is fragrant.

桃花似錦柳如烟

318. Tō|ka-wa nishiki-ni$_x$ ni, yanagi-wa kemuri-no$_x$ goto(shi.

The peach blossoms like brocade, the willows like smoke.

The spring vista of April. Reality as is, is the exquisite natural scenery of enlightenment.

棒頭有眼明如日

319. Bō|tō-ni manako$_x$ a(ri aki(raka-naru-koto hi-no$_x$ goto(shi.   (Zen 6)

The stick's end has an eye bright as the sun.

The excellent Zen general doesn't strike with a blind stick.

水自茫茫花自紅

320. Mizu-wa onozuka(ra bō|bō, hana-wa onozuka(ra kurenai-nari.   (Ox 9V)

Waters by nature are vast, flowers by nature are red.

Enlightenment's revelation, as well as the natural beauty of this earth, is all here in this. "Vast" refers to water's spreading far and wide.

求心歇處即無事

321. Gu|shin ya(mu tokoro sunawa(chi bu|ji.   (Rinzai 1X)

The seeking mind come to rest: Nothing-doing.

When all wishful thinking ends you're open to the state of nothing-doing (true enlightenment). [See #43.]

清風匝地有何極

322. Sei|fū sō|chi nan-no$_2$ kiwama(ri-ka$_3$ a(ran$_1$.   (Cliff 1V)

A clear breeze sweeps the earth—around what pivot?

The freshness of a cool breeze over the whole earth. It's not that the rest of the world isn't cool and refreshing.

滿架薔薇一院香

323. Man|ka-no shō|bi ichi|in kamba(shi.

A trellis-full of thorny roses suffuses the temple with fragrance.

The fragrance of a whole lattice-full of roses blooming spreads throughout the temple. An exquisite image for the present's completeness.

無角鐵牛眠少室

324. Mu|kaku-no tetsu|gyū Shō|shitsu-ni$_x$ nemu(ru.

The hornless iron bull sleeps on Shōshitsu.

The way Daruma Daishi [Bodhidharma] sat in Zen in Shōrin-ji [-monastery]. The solid state of mind with no crevice for so much as a hair of discrimination to enter.

無限輪鎚擊不開

325. Kagi(ri$_x$ na(ki rin|tsui u(te-domo hira(ke[zu.   (Cliff 9V)

Without a break, hard swung hammer blows—can't open its gates.

This bespeaks the solid strength of our Buddha-nature.

爲君幾下蒼龍窟

326. Kimi-ga$_x$ tame-ni iku(tabi-ka sō|ryū-no$_2$ kutsu-ni$_3$ kuda(ru$_1$.   (Cliff 3V)

For you going down—countless times—into the sea dragon's cave.

For the sake of this Way, how many times have I risked my life in bone-crushing labors! "You": The Buddha-Dharma.

狸奴白牯放毫光

327. Ri|nu byak|ko gō|kō-o$_x$ hana(tsu.   (Eye 1)

The raccoon dog and the white bull emanate an intense light.

Seen with the Buddhas' eye, both raccoon dog [sly and tipsy] and white bull [the sacred cow of India] —all beings—are Buddhas.

獅子教兒迷子訣

328. Shi|shi ji-ni$_x$ oshi(yu mei|shi-no ketsu.   (Mu 15V)

The lion teaches its cubs with the "lost child" dodge.

The parallel case of a beloved disciple made to make a journey.

珊瑚枝枝撐著月

329. San|go|shi|shi tsuki-o_x tō|jaku-su.   (Cliff 100K,V)

The coral: Each branch sustains/reveals the moon.

Each branch of the coral holds up the moon. Each individual atom of dust, every detail of every thing, shines in the light.

白雲流水共悠悠

330. Haku|un ryū|sui tomo-ni yū|yū.   (Realm 5)

White clouds and flowing water, calm and eternal.

The exquisite vista free of all ideas and motives. Calm and eternal: Far-seeing and far-reaching. ["Unsui": Monk.]

白雲斷處家山妙

331. Haku|un ta(yuru tokoro ka|san myō-nari.   (Eye 3)

When the white clouds are broken up
The mountains of home stand out mysteriously.

When delusions disappear, enlightenment's fine vista is revealed.

百尺竿頭坐底人

332. Hyaku|shaku kan|tō-ni za-suru tei-no hito.   (Mu 46K)

A guy sitting on top of a pole a hundred feet high.

He's stuck in a stage of realization, not knowing how to go ahead. With his rear end planted on one level of enlightenment he's useless.

百花春至爲誰開

333. Hyak|ka haru ita(tte ta-ga_x tame-ni-ka hira(ku.   (Cliff 5V)

Hundreds of flowers: Spring comes—for whom do they bloom?

For the sake of how many people do the spring flowers open? The mystery of the underlying permanent reality/self-and-other.

盡大地藏身無處

334. Jin|daiji mi-o_x kaku(su-ni tokoro_x [nashi].   (Mu 20V)

In all the great earth—there's no place his body is hidden.

His body's hiding place is every place; its glorious light fills all places everywhere.

知音知後更誰知

335. Chi|in shi(tte nochi sara-ni tare-ka shi(ran.

Intimate friends know; after them, who will know?

These inmost thoughts intimate comrades know about aren't even understood by anyone else.

48

絶學無爲閑道人

336. Zetsu|gaku mu|i-no kan|dō|nin.　(Song 1:1)

Having cut out learning, without doings, the leisurely man of the Way.

The true man of the Way who's got free of the dirt of enlightenment. Cut out learning: Get to the bottom of the Buddha's Way, cutting your way into it. Without doings: Without aversions or illusions, live out your destiny free and unconcerned.

翻手作雲覆手雨

337. Te-o$_x$ hirugae(seba kumo-to$_x$ na(ri te-o$_x$ kutsugae(seba ame.　(Táng [Dù Fǔ])

With a flick of the hand make clouds; drop the hand: Rain.

The able strength of a master is vast like this, but need not take such forms.

臘月蓮華拂拂香

338. Rō|getsu-no ren|ge futsu|futsu-to-shite kamba(shi.

December's lotus, breeze-blown, fragrant.

There are no lotuses in December [the Month of the Rat]. An image for free action detached from emotion and willfulness.

自笑一聲天地驚

339. Ji|shō is|sei ten|chi odoro(ku.　(Rinzai 3XIX)

I laugh once; the sound puts the heavens and the earth to fright.

The incongruity is unbearable. At one laugh the universe is startled.

落花流水甚茫茫

340. Rak|ka ryū|sui hanaha(da bō|bō.　(Cliff 25V)

Falling blossoms and flowing water: Very open and limitless.

Excellent activity without ideas or motives, naturally free of dependence on times and places, able to fit in any situation.

萬象之中獨露身

341. Ban|zō shi chū doku|ro|shin.　(Equanimity 64K)

In the myriad forms, a Single Body is revealed.

The real, changeless, alone-honored Buddha—how many of them are there?

萬里無雲孤月圓

342. Ban|ri kumo$_x$ na(ku ko|getsu mado(ka-nari.

Ten thousand miles without a cloud: The lone moon is full.

When it's clear enough and the moon is perfectly round, the heart, the moon solitary and full, mountains and rivers—all are bright. The subtle taste of the manifest present event.

Calligraphy, the 3rd and 4th characters, *Sei Fu* "pure breeze," of phrase #200, by Eido Roshi.

要識眞金火裏看

343. Shin|kin-o$_3$ shi(ran-to$_2$ yō(seba$_1$ ka|ri-ni mi(yo.   (Mu 20C)

If you want to know whether it's pure gold
  You must see it through fire.

By going through unrelieved suffering, distress and hardship, distinguish truth from error, wisdom from folly.

詩至重吟初見功

344. Shi-wa jū|gin-ni$_x$ ita(tte haji(mete kō-o$_x$ mi(ru.   (Equanimity)

When a poem gets the most serious possible recitation
  We first see its merit.

To the extent that a poem is worked over and polished, its flavor emerges. Discipline is also that way.

話盡山雲海月情

345. Kata(ri tsu(kusu san|un kai|getsu-no jō.   (Cliff 53V)

Words used up, the feeling of mountain clouds and the moon at sea.

Comrades of a mind talk together of all the natural beauty of what their mind is set on.

説似一物即不中

346. Setsu|ji ichi|motsu soku fu|chū.   (Platform)

Whatever I say would already be off target.

Nothing said or pointed out can hit the truth exactly. After all, it's the directness of Buddha-nature that hits the mark. Words of Nangaku Ejō Zenji.

誰家無明月清風

347. Ta-ga ie-ni-ka mei|getsu$_2$ sei|fū$_3$ na(karan$_1$.   (Cliff 6Kn)

Whose house is without bright moonlight and clear breezes?

Nowhere is there a place without bright moonlight and clear breezes. How many people can there be with no Buddha-nature?

謝三郎不知四字

348. Ja|san|rō shi|ji-o$_x$ shi(ra[zu.   (Mu 41C)

Jasanrō's not knowing four *kanji*.

A fisherman who didn't even know the four *kanji* used [for the date] on coins. This bespeaks non-knowledgeable, non-discriminating directness (the state of enlightenment, gone beyond discriminating between knowing and not knowing). Some say Jasanrō was simply a fisherman, others that he was the Venerable Gensha (who was the third ["san"] son ["-rō"] of the Ja family, and started out as a fisherman).

貴懸羊頭賣狗肉

349. Tatto(ku yō|tō-o$_x$ kaka(gete ku|niku-o$_x$ u(ru.   (Comprehensive 29)

Prominently display a sheep's head and sell dog meat.

To deceive people. The great difference between a pretentious sign and what's inside.

通身是病通身藥

350. Tsū|shin ko(re yamai tsū|shin kusuri.   (Jōwa 10 [Ummon])

The whole body being diseased, imbue the body with medicine.

Since the body *is* a mass of delusions, it's possible to become a Buddha—and to become diseased through and through.

遠山無限碧層層

351. En|zan kagi(ri$_x$ na(ki heki|sō|sō.   (Cliff 20V2)

Endlessly arising distant mountains, blue heaped upon blue.

The sentence as it stands—native natural beauty. Implied is the subtle charm of endless enlightenment. [This is Eido Roshi's translation of the phrase; see also #548.]

金剛正眼輝乾坤

352. Kon|gō-no shō|gen ken|kon-ni$_x$ kagaya(ku.

The diamond-true eye illumines the whole universe.

The penetrating eye of the excellent Zen monk enlightens the universe.

鐵壁銀山絕來往

353. Tep|peki gin|zan rai|ō-o zes(su.   (Realm 3)

Iron wall and silver mountain cut off coming and going.

Your mind in an inaccessible, high place—attached to not even a single person.

鐵樹花開二月春

354. Tetsu|ju hana hira(ku ni|gatsu-no haru.   (Zen 8)

The iron tree's flowers open in the second month in spring.

—an expression of the freedom of enlightenment. The excellent action of no-mind. The spring scenery of subtle insight. [The second lunar month: March–April.]

隨分著衣喫飯去

355. Bun-ni$_x$ shitaga(tte jaku|e kip|pan-shi sa(ru.   (Zen)

Take what you deserve: Put on robes, eat the food and leave.

Each person does his own part. Adapting to situations, make yourself their master.

雨後青山青轉青

雨後青山青轉青

356. U|go-no sei|zan sei utata sei.

After rain, blue-green mountains, blue after blue.

A single layer of greenish-blue—beautiful. And, the samādhi of differentiation (the state of mind where each mountain stands out from the rest and yet they form a single sheet).

雨竹風松皆説禪

357. U|chiku fū|shō mina Zen-o$_x$ to(ku.   (Daie)

Rain on the bamboo, wind in the pines—all preach Zen.

The bamboo wet with rain, the pines swaying in the wind—all are the great Dharma discourse of Zen.

雪上加霜又一重

358. Setsu|jō shimo-o$_x$ kuwa(u mata ichi jū.   (Cliff 78Vn)

On top of the snow, add a further layer of frost.

A pointless business. There's already plenty. Absurd.

電光石火存機變

359. Den|kō sek|ka ki|hen-o$_x$ son(su.   (Cliff 26V)

In lightning's glare, at flint's spark:
    Each instant, dwell in action according to circumstances.

In a flash, an instant—swift-changing action in response to opportunity. The excellent Zen monk's splendid capability.

頭頭全露法王身

360. Zu|zu matta(ku hō|ō|shin-o$_x$ ara(wasu.

Every thing perfectly reveals the body of the sovereign Dharma.

All the myriad things are the embodiment of the Dharma. Since you're actually Buddha, you can bow to each tree and blade of grass.

飢來喫飯冷添衣

361. U(e kita(reba han-o$_x$ kis(shi hi(yureba e-o$_x$ so(u.   (Chūhō)

When hunger comes I eat rice, when cold I put on another robe.

The fine and free state of the perfected man who rests in his destiny, totally at ease, with nothing on his mind. The excellent activity of no-mind.

飢來喫飯困來眠

362. U(e kita(reba han-o$_x$ kis(shi kon-ji kita(reba nemu(ru.   (Rinzai 1XXII)

When hunger comes, I eat rice; when fatigue comes, I sleep.

The fine and free state of the perfected man who rests in his destiny, totally at ease, with nothing on his mind. The excellent activity of no-mind.

黒漆桶裏盛黒汁

363. Koku|shit|tsū|ri-ni koku|jū-o$_x$ mo(ru.　　(Realm 1)

The black lacquer pail is full of black liquid.

Add black to black. Everyone on one level, not ranked or opposed. The direct, open quality of impartiality. And, indefinite: Not cut-and-dried.

EIGHT

一日不作一日不食

364. Ichi|jitsu na(sa[za(reba ichi|jitsu ku(rawa[zu.　　(ZFZB I83)

On a day you don't work, that day don't eat.

Hyakujō Zenji's famous words. They help us hold carefully to religious self-discipline, not to vegetate in an idle life. This is the main purpose of outdoor work for the Zen monastic community. In this happy expression we see Hyakujō Zenji's great dynamic skill in action.

三界無法何處求心

365. San|kai|mu|hō, izu(re-no tokoro-ni-ka shin-o$_x$ moto(men.　　(Cliff 37K,V; Realm 5:15)

In the three realms there's no Dharma; where to search for the mind?

Everything in the three realms (of desire, of form, and formless—worlds of delusion) appears in no fixed form or place. Where could what we arbitrarily call "mind" be? But that mis-taken thing is *some*thing.

上無諸佛下無衆生

366. Kami sho|butsu$_x$ na(ku, shimo shu|jō$_x$ na(shi.

Above, no Buddhas
　Below, no beings.

Enlightenment's direct "Fundamentally, not a thing exists."

不入虎穴爭得虎兒

367. Ko|ketsu-ni$_x$ ira[zu(mba ika(de-ka ko|ji-o$_x$ e(n.　　(Cliff 26Kc)

If you don't go into the tiger's cave
　How can you get a tiger cub?

In the life of Zen practice, when you stop striving in the way of discrimination, you're ready for insight into your nature.

前無釋迦後無彌勒

368. Mae-ni Sha|ka$_x$ na(ku, shirie-ni Mi|roku$_x$ na(karan.　　(Mu 37C)

Before you there has been no Shākya
　After you there will be no Maitreya.

If you act on the basis of enlightenment's First Principle, there is no "before" and there is no "after". There is no Shākya[muni, the "sage of the Shākya clan," the historical Buddha]; there is no Maitreya [the future Buddha, benevolent, invincible]. This very time, this very place, this very matter—is the entire body, complete and perfect, of Shākya, of Maitreya.

凡聖同居龍蛇混雜

369. Bon|shō dō|go, ryū|da kon|zatsu.　(Cliff 35K)

The worldly and holy live together,
　Dragons and snakes in a tangle.

Ordinary people and Buddhas, anybody and everybody, are in an indiscriminate mix. That's the wonder of the way it is.

南山起雲北山下雨

370. Nan|zan-ni kumo-o$_x$ oko(shi, hoku|san-ni ame-o$_x$ kuda(su.　(Cliff 83K; Realm 5:19)

South mountain gathers clouds
　North mountain draws down rain.

This is an expression of the covenant among all things to mutually reflect each other with no interference.

參須實參悟須實悟

371. San-wa subekara(ku jis|san-narubeshi.
　　Go-wa subekara(ku jitsu go-narubeshi.　(Mu 4C)

Practice has got to be whole-hearted practice.
　Realization has got to be true realization.

True practice—real, thorough mastery—is altogether priceless. Practicing only for appearance's sake, without a sense of moral consequences, one can't hope for real enlightenment.

古洞風清寒潭月皎

372. Ko|dō kaze kiyo(ku, kan|tan tsuki shiro(shi.

The ancient cavern's breeze is fresh
　The spring-fed pool's moon is bright.

The subtle scene evident here and now. The natural beauty that is the state of mind of Great Enlightenment.

君子愛財取之以道

373. Kun|shi-wa zai-o$_x$ ai-suru-mo, kore-o$_x$ to(ru-ni michi-o$_x$ mot(te-su.

The wise love wealth—to get it for use in the right Way.

The sage receives wealth too—but never selfishly, by way of unfair dealings. He cares about assets without being grasping.

四十九年一字不説

374. Shi|jū|ku|nen ichi|ji fu|setsu.

Forty-nine years and not a single word said.

Speaking on the basis of the First Principle [of enlightenment], even the Dharma teaching of the Buddha's whole lifetime is to be taken as "not a single word spoken".

54

大用現前不存軌則

375. Tai|yū gen|zen, ki|soku-o$_x$ son(se[zu.   (Ummon 2)

The great need right before your eyes
  Doesn't let you keep on going by rules.

The action of one of great enlightenment is free of all restraints and obstacles, going beyond the rules because the rules no longer apply.

大道無門千差有路

376. Dai|dō mu|mon, sen|sa michi$_x$ a(ri.   (Mu Preface, V)

The great Way with no entrance gates:
  There are thousands of different ways in.

The great Dào is open wide in all directions: You have free access by way of *any* route.

天上天下唯我獨尊

377. Ten|jō ten|ka yui|ga doku|son.   (Cliff 57K)

In heaven above and under heaven, only I alone am honored.

The lion's roar of the World-honored One [Shākyamuni Buddha] just after his birth [i.e., enlightenment]. The miracle of one newborn and standing alone with no companion.

如擊石火似閃電光

378. Geki|sek|ka-no$_x$ goto(ku, sen|den|kō-ni$_x$ ni(tari.   (Compendium 7)

Like fire off flint, bright as flashing lightning.

Refers to sharp dynamism, exceedingly fine and swift.

如龍得水似虎靠山

379. Ryū-no$_2$ mizu-o$_4$ u(ru-ga$_3$ goto(ku$_1$, tora-no$_2$ yama-ni$_4$ yo(ru-ni$_3$ ni(tari$_1$.
(Cliff 8I, 9Kc, 31I)

Like the dragon risen with its water element
  Like the tiger that's taken to the mountains.

The state of splendid, awesome dignity manifest in the actions of the excellent Zen monk. Sometimes, to "seize the time".

好雪片片不落別處

380. Kō|setsu hem|pen bes|sho-ni$_x$ o(chi[zu.   (Cliff 42K; Realm 4)

A good snow: Snow flakes—none fall out of place.

With enough one-by-one snowflakes for a good snow, where does each fall? Look: The miracle of being becoming!

官不容針私通車馬

381. Kan-ni-wa hari-o-mo$_x$ i(re[zu, watakushi-ni-wa sha|ba-o-mo$_x$ tsū(zu.   (Rinzai 3XIX)

Officially, not room for a needle; privately, horse and carriage pass in.

Not public, facile twisting and distortion of the Dharma, but toleration of what comes "by the back way". The freedom of action that by turns says thoroughly "no" when it's time for denial, completely "yes" when it's time for affirmation.

心外無法満目青山

382. Shin|ge mu|hō, mam|moku sei|zan.   (Lamp 25)

Outside the mind there is no Dharma; everywhere, blue mountains.

—since mind and surroundings are one.

快人一言快馬一鞭

383. Kai|jin-no ichi|gen, kai|ba-no ichi|ben.   (Compendium)

The keen man at a word, the keen horse at a flick.

One word skilfully does another out of his doubt and confusion; one touch of the whip skilfully sets a horse to running.

應無所住而生其心

384. Ō mu sho jū ni shō go shin.   (Diamond 10)

Dwell nowhere, and so then realize THIS mind.

On the point of being without anything to dwell on, let this here-and-now mind happen. Get this mind that stays nowhere to develop! Set the mind that's attached to nothing whatsoever in action! Be satisfied without clinging. Action independent of ideas and motives.

把定要津壁立萬仞

385. Yō|shin-o$_x$ ha|jō-shite heki|ryū ban|jin.   (Rinzai Preface)

Guarding the vital ford—a wall going up twenty miles.

Having captured the essential point, keep the enemy at bay.

朝到西天暮歸東土

386. Ashita-ni Sei|ten-ni$_x$ ita(ri, kure-ni Tō|do-ni$_x$ kae(ru.

Mornings he gets to the Western Heaven
Evenings he comes home to the Eastern Land.

This refers to the Zen monk's unrestricted, excellent activity, his mind free of attachments. The Western Heaven is India; the Eastern Land, China. The subtle taste of freedom from time and space.

朝打三千暮打八百

387. Chō|da san|zen, bo|da hap|pyaku.   (Cliff 60Vn)

Mornings, blows—three thousand; evenings, blows—eight hundred.

The idea is repeated thrashing, beating, raining blows upon.

掀翻大海趯倒須彌

388. Dai|kai-o$_x$ kim|pon-shi, Shu|mi-o$_x$ teki|tō-su.　(Cliff 20I)

Lift, tip over the ocean; dance, kick over Mount Sumeru.

A metaphor for amazement at the able vigor of the excellent Zen monk.

教外別傳不立文字

389. Kyō|ge|betsu|den fu|ryū|mon|ji.　(Mu 6K)

Beyond teaching, a special transmission not fixed in words.

Enlightenment's fine-tune pointing is transmitted independently, going beyond the Buddha's teachings: It can't be expressed in words. [Followed by #400.]

李花不白桃花不紅

390. Ri|ka-wa shiro(kara[zu, tō|ka-wa kurenai-nara[zu.

Plum blossoms aren't white, peach blossoms aren't pink.

Beyond peach-pink and plum-white, a mysterious getting free of colors and shapes.

松老雲閒曠然自適

391. Matsu o(i kumo shizu(ka-ni-shite, kō|nen-to-shite ji|teki(su.　(Rinzai Preface)

Pine-old, cloud-quiet: Far-reaching, yet content by himself.

His state of mind like a pine grown old, like clouds quietly floating, he lives serenely, trusting to his selfless mind. The exquisite life of the leisurely man of the Way without doings.

桃李不言下自成蹊

392. Tō|ri-mono i(wa[za(re-domo shita onozuka(ra kei-o$_x$ na(su.

Peach and plum trees don't speak, but they get footpaths beneath them.

On the peach and plum trees are flowers and fruit—so, even though the trees don't beckon, men strive and contend beating paths to them. This is a metaphor: Though men of virtue neither discriminate nor are assertive, men naturally submit to them.

正法眼藏涅槃妙心

393. Shō|bō|gen|zō ne|han myō|shin.　(Mu 6K)

The Eye of the all-pervading True Dharma
The subtly marvelous Mind of Nirvāṇa.

"The Eye of the all-pervading True Dharma" is the real Dharma, whose radiance enlightens all—the treasury that holds all things. "The subtly marvelous Mind of Nirvāṇa" is unfathomably deep, finely subtle enlightenment at the heart's core.

氣吞佛祖眼蓋乾坤

394. Ki Bus|so-o$_x$ no(mi, manako ken|kon-o$_x$ ō(u.

Spirit swallowing Buddha and Patriarchs, eye covering heaven and earth.

The excellent Zen monks' spirit prevails. The true man without rank in action.

潛行密用如愚如魯

395. Sen|gō|mitsu|yū, gu-no$_x$ goto(ku ro-no$_x$ goto(shi.   (Mirror 91–2)

Hidden practice, secret function—as if simple, as if inept.

Inconspicuously, quietly and carefully practicing the Buddha's Way, it must seem to outsiders, if you don't intentionally act otherwise, that you are an utter fool. This is being one worthy to be called a true master among masters.

無説無聞是眞般若

396. Mu|setsu mu|mon ko(re shin-no han|nya.   (Cliff 6Vc)

Without speaking, without hearing—this is the true wisdom.

True prajñā, the wisdom of enlightenment that deliberately rises above everything.

狗子還有佛性也無

397. Ku|su-ni kae(tte bus|shō$_x$ a(ri-ya mata na(shi-ya.   (Mu 1K)

Has a dog Buddha-nature or not?

Is there Buddha-nature [capacity for enlightenment] even in a dog—or not? The famous "Mu" kōan of Jōshū Zenji: A monk asked, "Has a dog Buddha-nature or not?" Jōshū said, "Mu" [#14].

獅子一吼野干腦裂

398. Shi|shi ik|ku-sureba ya|kan nō|retsu-su.

The lion's one roar splits open wild offenders' brains.

At the sound of the ferocious lion's roar [the Buddha's preaching], the foxes tremble, thoroughly intimidated. One shout from the clear-eyed Founder [Rinzai], and all the students' nerve is crushed.

玉兔東昇金烏西墜

399. Gyoku|to higashi-ni nobo(ri, kin|u nishi-ni o(tsu.

The Jade Hare rises in the East, the Golden Crow sinks in the West.

The moon rises in the East, the sun sets in the West. A mysterious aspect of enlightenment as it is.

直指人心見性成佛

400. Jiki|shi nin|shin, ken|shō jō|butsu.

Points right at your mind:
  You see your true nature—become what you are: Buddha.

Not depending on dogmas and phrases, directly pointing to your own real intention—this is the root means of penetrating insight into your Buddha-nature, the attainment of Buddhahood (decisive peace of mind).

眞獅子兒善獅子吼

401. Shin-no shi|shi ji yo(ku shi|shi ku(su.   (Cliff 4Kn)

The real lion cub is good at roaring the lion's roar.

The excellent disciple is not inferior to his master. As might be expected, he is the lion's cub who did well.

眼似流星機如掣電

402. Manako-wa ryū|sei-no$_x$ goto(ku, ki-wa sei|den-no$_x$ goto(shi.   (Cliff 24I)

Eye like a shooting star, dynamism like lightning.

Glint of insight penetrating as a falling star, action quick as a lightning flash. Describes the excellent Zen monk's dynamic tact.

祖師心印七花八裂

403. So|shi-no shin|in shik|ka|hachi|retsu.

The Patriarch's mind seal: When seven flowers split into eight.

Freely taking the Great Way of Buddhas and Patriarchs, grind it to dust, and smash the enlightenment of the Patriarchs to smithereens too. [See #86.]

聲前一句千聖不傳

404. Shō|zen-no ik|ku, sen|shō fu|den.   (Cliff 7I, 90I)

Before there was a voice was the first phrase
 Which the thousand Holy Ones have not handed down.

"The first phrase before there were voices" is enlightenment's direct pointing. The Buddha couldn't preach about it, nor could the Patriarchs transmit it.

至道無難唯嫌揀擇

405. Shi|dō bu|nan, yui ken ken|jaku.   (Cliff 2K)

The perfect Way is clear of difficulties—only it bars preferences.

The great Way of the Buddhas and Patriarchs is not in the least a difficult thing, but if it is seen in antagonism, then whichever viewpoint or side you take, attached to it, your mind will never come awake.

色即是空空即是色

406. Shiki soku ze kū, kū soku ze shiki.   (Heart)

Form *is* śunyatā, śunyatā *is* form.

Form [appearance] is existence, differentiation; śunyatā [literally, emptiness] is non-existence, non-differentiation. Differentiation is exactly non-differentiation, non-differentiation precisely differentiation. Form and śunyatā are not two. The founder of our religion found that all actual beings have no fundamental self-nature, that is, they have no real existence except by way of causation and conditions.

萬法歸一一亦不守

407. Mam|pō itsu-ni$_x$ ki(su, itsu-mo mata mamo(ra[zu.   (Faith 21:4 and 11:2)

The myriad dharmas come down to the One, and that One won't last.

Don't stay with the blessing of enlightenment, go beyond the Absolute.

要行便行要坐便坐

408. Yu(kan-to$_x$ yō(seba sunawa(chi yu(ki, za(sen-to$_x$ yō(seba sunawa(chi za(su.

(Rinzai 1X)

If he's about to walk then he walks, if he's about to sit then he sits.

The true man without rank in action—acting freely, bound by no restrictions at all.

身心脱落脱落身心

409. Shin|jin datsu|raku, datsu|raku shin|jin.   (Realm 5)

Body, mind shed, drop; shed, drop body, mind.

Freeing both body and mind of all distressing delusions, enlightenment is attained; because the free body and mind shed delusions anew, all beings are saved from suffering. The former is the quest for *bodhi* [great enlightenment]; the latter is the fulfillment of the man of great enlightenment, to enlighten all beings.

逢佛殺佛逢祖殺祖

410. Hotoke-ni$_x$ at(te-wa Hotoke-o$_x$ koro(shi, So-ni$_x$ at(te-wa So-o$_x$ koro(su.

(Rinzai 1XVIIIc)

Meeting Buddha, kill the Buddha
  Happening on a Patriarch, slay that Patriarch.

Brave, devoted practice. Not until you're through with killing can you live in peace—and yet the true man of the Way succeeds in overcoming the Buddhas and the Patriarchs.

金屑雖貴落眼成翳

411. Kin|setsu tatto(shi-to$_x$ iedo(mo manako-ni$_x$ o(chite ei-to$_x$ na(ru.   (Zen 8; Rinzai 2XII)

Gold dust, though precious, getting in the eyes becomes a dark blur.

Enlightenment really is priceless, but if you get attached to it, it becomes an illusion. A metaphor for the grime of enlightenment that's not been got rid of.

銀盌盛雪明月藏鷺

412. Gin|wan-ni yuki-o$_x$ mo(ri, mei|getsu-ni ro-o$_x$ kaku(su.   (Mirror 5,6)

The silver bowl full of snow, the moonlight hiding the egret.

Seeming the same, different; looking different, the same. This equality discriminating and differentiation equating is an illustration of the wondrous mystery of "not one, not two".

60

隨處作主立處皆眞

413. Zui|sho-ni shu-to_x na(reba, ris|sho mina shin-nari. (Rinzai 1XVI)

In accord with situations be their master
  And every place you stand is right.

Whatever the circumstances, don't lose your independence, so that every place you go becomes the real world.

雲月是同溪山各異

414. Un|getsu ko(re ona(ji, kei|zan onoono kotona(ru. (Equanimity 35K; Mu 35V)

The moon in the clouds is the same moon;
  Each of the mountains and streams is different.

There is only one moon in the sky above, but its appearance differs depending on the place you view it from. Variety within identity.

鞍上無人鞍下無馬

415. An|jō hito_x na(ku, an|ka uma_x na(shi.

On the saddle no man, under the saddle no horse.

There is neither man riding nor horse ridden. This refers to samādhi: Complete union of the mind free of thought in the one "suchness," the fundamental unity of the World. This is the essence of horseback riding.

頭上漫漫脚下漫漫

416. Zu|jō mam|man kyak|ka mam|man. (Cliff 27Vn)

Endless immensity overhead, endless immensity under feet.

Full of the sky and also of the ground.

龍吟雲起虎嘯風生

417. Ryū gin(zureba kumo oko(ri, tora usobu(keba kaze shō(zu. (Changes)

With the dragon's hum, clouds rise; with the tiger's roar, the wind stirs.

The intense energy of dragon and tiger. A metaphor for the excellence in action of the Zen monk.

TEN

一句定乾坤　一劒平天下

418. Ik|ku ken|kon-o_x sada(me, ik|ken ten|ka-o_x taira(gu.

One thing said sends the heavens and the earth into samādhi;
  One sword subdues everything under the sun.

After enlightenment, one word, one hint, pierces through heaven and earth.

一峰雲片片　雙澗水潺潺

419. Ip|pō kumo hem|pen, sō|kan mizu zen|zen.　(Realm 1)

A single peak's clouds: Buttermilk sky
Its two valleys' streams murmur on.

A subtle meaning is revealed by the clouds with no mind to float floating, the waters with no mind to flow able to be flowing.

一華開五葉　結果自然成

420. Ik|ka go|yō-o$_x$ hira(ki, kek|ka ji|nen-ni na(ru.

One flower opens: Five petals—forming fruit that ripens on its own.

When the flower: The mind—blooms into the five discriminations [senses], the fruit: Buddhahood—is realized spontaneously.

一點梅花蕊　三千世界香

421. It|ten bai|ka-no zui, san|zen|se|kai kamba(shi.

One dot of plum-blossom bud
And the thousands of worlds fill with fragrance.

The wonderful flower that is the One Mind sends forth fragrance, even to the great universe of billions of space-time worlds.

不知何處寺　風送鐘聲來

422. Shi(ra[zu izu|ko-no tera-zo, kaze shō|sei-o$_x$ oku(ri kita(ru.

No telling where the temple is—the wind carries the bell's sound here.

The quiet dimness and calm feeling of evening near dark; this, before your eyes, as it is, is the miraculous "taste" of enlightenment.

世尊不説説　迦葉不聞聞

423. Se|son fu|setsu-no setsu, Ka|shō fu|mon-no mon.　(Zen 7)

The World-honored One spoke without speaking;
Kāśyapa heard without hearing.

The World-honored One [the Buddha] holding up a flower in his fingers and Kāśyapa smiling [at the sight of it]—a profoundly subtle interaction.

九夏寒岩雪　三冬枯木花

424. Kyū|ka kan|gan-no yuki, san|tō ko|boku-no hana.　(Realm 2)

Through ninety days of summer, the exposed crag's snow;
Through three months of winter, the decayed tree's flowers.

Snow of the real summer, flowers of true winter. The state of absolute freedom after enlightenment. The mind clear, even fire is cool.

62

佛殿裏燒香　山門頭合掌

425. Butsu|den|ri-ni shō|kō-shi, sam|mon tō-ni gas|shō-su.　(Realm 1)

Burn incense in the Buddha Hall, gasshō in front of the monastery gate.

These are monks' regular duties, forms that should be a matter of course. Gasshō: (Give) a palms-together greeting. [Literally, "mountain gate"—since most Chinese Zen monasteries were in the mountains.]

來說是非者　便是是非人

426. Kita(tte ze|hi-o$_x$ to(ku mono-wa, sunawa(chi ko(re ze|hi-no hito.　(Mu 18V)

Those who come to talk right-and-wrong
 Are the very ones who *are* right and wrong.

Those who are always sticklers about right and wrong in others never, when all is said and done, get past being right-and-wrong people.

兀然無事坐　春來草自生

427. Kotsu|nen-to-shite bu|ji-ni-shite za-sureba,
 Shun|rai kusa onozuka(ra shō(zu.

Steadfastly doing nothing, sitting there
 Spring comes and the grass sprouts of itself.

Just sit zazen, and some day the time of insight will have to come.

兩頭俱截斷　一劍倚天寒

428. Ryō|tō tomo-ni setsu|dan-shite, ik|ken ten-ni$_x$ yot(te susama(ji.　(Realm 1)

The double heads cut asunder, the sword is so miraculously
 [Sharp it makes you—as does the power of] Heaven—shiver!

The dualities of existence, delusion and enlightenment too, utterly cut down and swept away—sit calmly in the one real truth.

出門逢釋迦　入門逢彌勒

429. Mon-o$_x$ i(dete-wa Sha|ka-ni$_x$ a(i, mon-ni$_x$ i(tte-wa Mi|roku-ni$_x$ a(u.

Go out through the gate: Meet Shākyamuni;
 Go in through the gate: Meet Maitreya.

Seen greatly enlightened, burly men and flower children are all Shākyamuni [the historical Buddha] and Amitābha [the Buddha of boundless light]. [Maitreya is the Buddha to come.]

十年歸不得　忘却來時道

430. Jū|nen kae(ru-koto-o e[za(reba, rai|ji-no$_2$ michi-o$_3$ bō|kyaku-su$_1$.　(Hán-shān 5)

For ten years I haven't had to go back; I forget the way I came.

Having trained for many years, enlightenment!—and end up having forgotten that enlightenment too.

十方無處空　大地無寸土

431.　Jip|pō ko|kū$_x$ na(ku, dai ji sun|do$_x$ na(shi.　(Comprehensive 27)

The ten quarters without a place that's empty
The whole world without an inch of land.

In the whole world of an intensely concentrated mind, where can an inch of ground be seen?

十方薄伽梵　一路涅槃門

432.　Jip|pō Bo|gya|han, ichi ro ne|han|mon.

The ten directions: The Bhagavān; the One Way: Nirvāṇa's gate.

The ten quarters [of space: in the directions of the eight compass points, nadir and zenith] all around are the body, right before you, of the Buddha. This very place is the only path to the Buddha's Realm.

只在此山中　雲深不知處

433.　Tada ko(no$_2$ san|chū-ni$_3$ a(ri$_1$, kumo fuka(u-shite tokoro-o$_x$ shi(ra[zu.　(Táng)

Only dwell in these mountains—
The clouds so thick there's no telling where.

When a man of high character goes into the mountains, his whereabouts are not easily known. His mind's nature becomes clarity, though the eye can't see it.

只許老胡知　不許老胡會

434.　Tada Rō|ko-no$_2$ chi-o$_3$ yuru(shite$_1$, Rō|ko-no$_2$ e-o$_3$ yuru(sa[zu$_1$.　(Cliff 1Vc, Mu 9C)

Only granted that the Old Barbarian knows,
Not that the Old Barbarian is imbued.

He knows about it, but I won't let you say he's made it part of himself. The Old Barbarian [i.e., foreigner] is Bodhidharma.

古松談般若　幽鳥弄眞如

435.　Ko|shō han|nya-o$_x$ dan(ji, yu|chō shin|nyo-o$_x$ rō(su.　(Eye)

Anciently, the pines speak Wisdom; profoundly, the birds chatter Thusness.

Even waterfowl and groves of trees are the chanting of the Buddha's name and of the Dharma. The true Buddha-Dharma fills your eyes, fills your ears. [Wisdom:hannya:prajñā::Thusness:shinnyo: bhūtatathatā::English:Sino-Japanese:Sanskrit.]

吾心似秋月　碧潭清皎潔

436.　Wa(ga kokoro shū|getsu-ni$_x$ ni(tari, heki|tan kiyo(u-shite kō|ketsu.　(Hán-shān)

My mind like the harvest moon,
A deep jade-green clear pool
Glistening pure white.

My mind is like the bright moonlight of autumn, its untouched serene purity on the surface of the water.

君看此花枝　中有風露香

437. Kimi mi(yo ko(no ka|shi, naka-ni fū|ro-no$_2$ kamba(shiki$_3$ a(ri$_1$.

You gaze on this flowering branch
Within is the fragrance of wind and dew.

The flowering branch is a metaphor for the mind; the fragrance of the wind and dew for its subtly marvelous universality [beyond discrimination].

坐水月道場　修空華萬行

438. Sui|getsu-no$_2$ dō|jō-ni$_3$ za(shi$_1$, kū|ge-no$_2$ man|gyō-o$_3$ shū-su$_1$.

Sitting with the moon in the water as your seat of practice
Cultivating flowers in the air as your myriad disciplines.

Both the moon reflected in the water and illusory flowers [spots] before your eyes are metaphors for the wonderful effect of play. The marvelous world of the master in action, not confining himself to set forms of practice.

夜來風雨聲　花落知多少

439. Ya|rai fū|u-no koe, hana otsu(ru-koto shi(nnu ta|shō-zo.　(Táng [Mèng Hào-rán])

At night came the sound of wind and rain;
Flowers have fallen, and I know there are many.

When the wind and rain are heavy during the night, a great many flowers will have fallen. A subtle aspect of enlightenment as it is.

好事不出門　惡事行千里

440. Kō|ji mon-o$_x$ i(de[zu, aku|ji sen|ri-o$_x$ yu(ku.

Good deeds never get out the door
Bad deeds go thousands of miles.

Virtuous deeds don't readily get around; the evil ones become widely known in no time.

始隨芳草去　又逐落花回

441. Hajime-wa hō|sō-ni$_x$ shitaga(tte sa(ri, mata rak|ka-o$_x$ o(ute kae(ru.　(Cliff 36K,V)

First I went out following fragrant grasses
And then I came back along with fallen blossoms.

Practice, being of no mind [to practice]—work, without intending to work—a marvelous life.

宇宙無双日　乾坤只一人

442. U|chū sō|jitsu$_x$ na(ku, ken|kon tada ichi|nin.

Under the sky—in the air—there are not two suns;
In heaven and on earth, there is but one man.

The state of the greatly awakened man: Standing alone, honored alone.

寒雲抱幽石　霜月照清池

443. Kan|un yū|seki-o$_x$ ida(ki, sō|getsu sei|chi-o$_x$ tera(su.　(Realm 6:5V)

The wintry clouds enfold the lone rock;
The frosty moon illumines the clear pool.

The attitude of the man of the Way of polished, indelible nobility—his subtle state of mind intense, awesome as a cool breeze.

山中無曆日　寒盡不知年

444. San|chū reki|jitsu$_x$ na(shi, kan tsu(kure-domo toshi-o$_x$ shi(ra[zu.　(Táng)

In the mountains there are no dates;
Winter over, there's no telling what year it is.

The life of the hermit is without Bon [a memorial festival in the summer] or New Year's; though winter comes and summer comes, months and days are unknown.

山花開似錦　澗水湛如藍

445. San|ka hira(ite nishiki-ni$_x$ ni(tari, kan|sui tata(ete ai-no$_x$ goto(shi. (Cliff 82K; Realm 4)

The autumn leaves open out like brocade
The stream's water clear, shadowed indigo.

The beauty of a mountain stream and its setting; the exquisite light-and-shadow scene of enlightenment that sees reality as it actually is. [Sanka: Literally, "mountain flowers".]

已見寒梅發　復聞啼鳥聲

446. Sude-ni kam|bai-no$_2$ hira(ku-o$_3$ mi$_1$, ma(ta tei|chō-no$_2$ koe-o$_3$ ki(ku$_1$.　(Táng)

Already you see the winter plum coming out
Again you hear the sound of calling birds.

The plum blooming, bush warblers singing—the feel and feeling of balmy spring days in a quiet retreat.

庵中閑打坐　白雲起峰頂

447. An|chū shizu(ka-ni ta|za(sureba, haku|un hō|chō-ni$_x$ oko(ru.　(Eye 1)

In the hut, calmly, I sit—and white clouds rise over the peak's summit.

The way the quiet life in the mountains is. An exquisite reflection of what's happening here and now.

張三喫鐵棒　李四忍疼痛

448. Chō|san tetsu|bō-o$_x$ kis(sureba, Ri|shi tō|tsū-o$_x$ shino(bu.

Zhāng's third son gets a taste of the iron rod
And Lǐ's fourth son bears the aching pain.

Freedom of action after enlightenment. Zhāng's third son and Lǐ's fourth son are like John Doe and Richard Roe.

66

微風吹幽松　近聽聲愈好

449. Bi|fū yū|shō-o$_x$ fu(ku, chika(ku ki(keba koe iyoiyo yo(shi.　(Hán-shān 5)

A light breeze in the lone pine—draw close to hear the sound better.

The subtle charm right before your eyes. The fine state of mind of one who's made it.

心隨萬境轉　轉處實能幽

450. Shin-wa ban|kyō-ni$_x$ shitaga(tte ten(zu, ten|jo jitsu-ni yo(ku yū-nari.

(Lamp 2; Rinzai 1XVIIId)

The mind goes with the infinity of situations, changing;
The result of change is truly, strongly mysterious.

The mind's working is causally bound to innumerable situations, but the true, full reality of enlightenment as it is transcends the innumerable situations.

懷州牛喫禾　益州馬腹張

451. Kai|shū-no ushi ka-o$_x$ kis(sureba, Eki|shū-no uma hara fuku(ru.

If in Huái District an ox gets into the crops
In Yì District a horse's belly distends.

Enlightenment's surpassing freedom in action. Once the self is forgotten, the universe is one.

扶過斷橋水　伴歸無月村

452. Tasu(kete-wa dan|kyō-no$_2$ mizu-o$_3$ su(gi$_1$,
Tomona(tte-wa mu|getsu-no$_2$ mura-ni$_3$ kae(ru$_1$.　(Mu 44C)

It supports you crossing the river when the bridge is down;
It keeps you company going back to your village when there's no moon.

—praise for the virtues of the staff. The state of detachment, freedom.

掬水月在手　弄花香滿衣

453. Mizu-o$_x$ kiku(sureba tsuki te-ni$_x$ a(ri, hana-o$_x$ rō(sureba kō e-ni$_x$ mi(tsu.　(Kidō)

Hold water, and the moon is in your hands;
Fondle flowers, and the fragrance suffuses your robes.

If you scoop up water in your hands it becomes *water*, if you hold a flower it becomes *the* flower. The mental state of one continual miracle, a kind of absorption free of habitual thought. The wonderful effect of all-pervading enlightenment.

採菊東籬下　悠然見南山

454. Kiku-o$_2$ tō|ri-no$_3$ moto-ni$_4$ to(tte$_1$, yū|zen-to-shite nan|zan-o$_x$ mi(ru.　(Comprehensive)

Gathering mums within the eastern bamboo fence
Distantly gazing at the southern hills.

The mental state of the man of great calm who has got free of the Buddha's Dharma and the norms of the times alike.

春眠不覺曉　處處聞啼鳥

455. Shum|min akatsuki-o $_x$ obo(e[zu, sho|sho tei|cho-o $_x$ ki(ku.　(Táng [Mèng Hào-rán])

Spring: Sleeping, not awake to the dawn—
　Everywhere I hear birds chirping.

Refers to the charm of a spring dawn, full of tangled feelings. [Followed by #439.]

春色無高下　花枝自短長

456. Shun|shoku kō|ge $_x$ na(ku. Ka|shi onozuka(ra tan|chō.　(Comprehensive 11)

Spring colors are not bright or subdued;
　A flowering branch is naturally short or long.

Differentiation within sameness. One's superior is the superior Dharmakāya, one's inferior is the inferior Dharmakāya [the embodiment of the Dharma].

月到中秋滿　風從八月涼

457. Tsuki-wa chū|shū-ni $_x$ ita(tte mi(chi, kaze-wa hachi|gatsu $_x$ yo(ri suzu(shi.　(Realm 4)

The moon gets to mid-autumn full
　The wind that comes with August is cool.

—the way that marvelous condition is, as if it were right in front of you.

月知明月秋　花知一樣春

458. Tsuki-wa mei|getsu-no $_2$ aki-o $_3$ shi(ri $_1$, hana-wa ichi|yō-no $_2$ haru-o $_3$ shi(ru $_1$.

The moon knows the autumn with its bright moon
　The flower knows the spring with its flowers all alike.

Things like the moon and flowers, though they are of no mind to, change naturally with time.

月落潭無影　雲生山有衣

459. Tsuki o(chite tan-ni kage $_x$ [naku], kumo shō(jite yama-ni e $_x$ a(ri.　(Eye)

The moon sets—the pool's without a trace
　Clouds appear—the mountains have robes.

The first line is the śunyatā aspect (the world of "there is not"), the second the form aspect (the world of existence)—and, a wonderful vista of insight into the present event as it is.

松樹千年翠　不入時人意

460. Shō|ju sen[nen-no midori, toki-no $_2$ hito-no $_3$ kokoro-ni $_4$ i(ra[zu $_1$.

The pine trees' thousands-of-years blue-gray green—
　Doesn't enter into the thinking of men of today.

Even the ceaseless true Dharma preaching of the pine is not heard by one who doesn't put his mind to it.

松無古今色　竹有上下節

461. Matsu-ni ko|kon-no$_2$ iro$_3$ na(ku$_1$, take-ni jō|ge-no$_2$ fushi$_3$ a(ri$_1$.

Pines are without [different] ancient and present colors;
　On bamboo there are, up and down, joints.

Invariance and difference. Without changing their own nature, they reveal the mystery of the truth as it is.

林下十年夢　湖邊一笑新

462. Rin|ka jū|nen-no yume, ko|hen is|shō arata-nare.

In the forest depths, ten years of dreams;
　At the lake's edge, one laugh: Surprise!

Having undergone ten years of hardship, achieving success, today Great Enlightenment is fully matured.

枯木倚寒巖　三冬無暖氣

463. Ko|boku kan|gan-ni$_x$ yo(ru, san|tō dan|ki$_x$ [nashi].

The withered tree leans against the cold precipice
　Three months of winter without a breath of warmth.

Like a dead tree or cold ashes, completely cut off, dead to: The viewpoint of death with no breath yet stirring.

此夜一輪滿　清光何處無

464. Ko(no yo ichi|rin mi(teri sei|kō izure-no tokoro-ni-ka na(karan.　　(Kidō 8)

Tonight the one disk fills the whole world with pure light—
　Is there any place that lacks it?

"Trusting in the full moon" signifies that there is no place where the spiritual light of absolute truth does not reach.

歸來坐虛室　夕陽在吾西

465. Kae(ri kita(tte kyo|shitsu-ni$_x$ za(sureba, seki|yō wa(ga$_2$ nishi-ni$_3$ a(ri$_1$.

Coming back to sit in the empty room, the evening sun is to my west.

To have awakened is no extraordinary thing. The excellent vista as it is—and, the subtle taste of no-mind.

水流元入海　月落不離天

466. Mizu naga(rete moto umi-ni$_x$ i(ri, tsuki o(chite ten-o$_x$ hana(re[zu.　　(Compendium)

Water flows from its source into the sea;
　The moon sets without leaving the sky.

Not to get separated from what is fundamental, even though the multifarious teachings are of uneven quality.

泣露千般草　吟風一樣松

467. Tsuyu-ni_x na(ku sem|pan-no kusa, kaze-ni_x gin(zu ichi|yō-no matsu.　(Hán-shān 1)

Weeping dew: All kinds of grasses;
  Moaning wind: All alike, pines.

All are subtle appearances of the here-and-now sort, enlightenment's subtle pointing.

流水寒山路　深雲古寺鐘

468. Ryū|sui Kan|zan-no michi, shin|un ko|ji-no kane.

Flowing water: Cold Mountain's path;
  Thick cloud: The ancient temple's bell!

The subtle charm deep in the mountains. Reality, as it is, is the mystery of enlightenment.

清風拂明月　明月拂清風

469. Sei|fū mei|getsu-o_x hara(i, mei|getsu sei|fū-o_x hara(u.　(Eye 1)

The clear breeze wipes away the bright moonlight
  The bright moonlight wipes away the clear breeze.

Substance becomes function—function, substance: They melt into each other perfectly, with no interference.

無風荷葉動　決定有魚行

470. Kaze_x na(ki-ni ka|yō ugo(ku, ketsu|jō-shite uo-no₂ yu(ku-koto₃ a(ran₁.
(Lamp 23; Zen 12 [Ummon])

No wind, but the lotus leaves move—must be a fish passing.

Dharma-nature [the reality behind all phenomena] is without characteristics—nevertheless, it manifests itself in forms. It is invisible, but clearly there.

牛飲水成乳　蛇飲水成毒

471. Ushi-no no(mu mizu-wa chichi-to_x na(ri, hebi-no no(mu mizu-wa doku-to_x na(ru.

The cow drinks water that becomes milk;
  The snake drinks water that becomes venom.

Water, the same substance, emerges as different things. The truth, which is one, manifests differently in each and every thing.

獨坐幽篁裡　彈琴復長嘯

472. Doku|za yū|kō-no uchi, dan|kin ma(ta chō|shō.　(Táng [Wáng Wéi])

Alone he sits within the thick bamboo grove;
  Thrumming a guitar, he whistles along.

The leisurely man of the Way without doings, delighting in the wonderful condition of "pine-old, cloud-quiet".

玉向泥中潔　松經雪後貞

473. Tama-wa dei|chū-ni$_x$ muka(tte isagiyo(ku, matsu-wa setsu|go-o$_x$ he(te tei-nari.

A gem's facets in the mud: Clean—
　A pine's sinews after a snow: Firm.

Even in the mud a jewel doesn't get dirty, and even heavy snow doesn't change the pine's form and color. The Absolute Truth never changes, no matter what the circumstances.

盡大地是藥　那箇是自己

474. Jin|dai|ji ko(re kusuri, na|ko-ka ko(re ji|ko.　(Cliff 87K)

The whole world is medicine—so what is the self?

Since medicine and disease cure each other, the whole world is medicine; there is nothing else.

相逢相不識　共語不知名

475. Ai a(ute ai shi(ra[zu, tomo-ni kata(tte na-o$_x$ shi(ra[zu.　(Rinzai 1XVIIIh)

You meet him without recognizing him,
　Talk with him without knowing his name.

The true state of the man of the Way of no-mind, the master of the house [your own body]. ["Him": Your own true nature.]

秋風吹渭水　落葉滿長安

476. Shū|fū I|sui-o$_x$ fu(keba, raku|yō Chō|an-ni$_x$ mi(tsu.　(Kidō 1)

Fall winds blow on the Wèi's waters
　Falling leaves fill Cháng-ān.

An exquisite natural scene. When the mind's attitude opens, the world is full of the light of hope. [Cháng-ān, "Constant Peace," is on the River Wèi.]

空手把鋤頭　步行騎水牛

477. Kū|shu-ni-shite jo|tō-o$_x$ to(ri, ho|kō-ni-shite sui|gyū-ni$_x$ no(ru.　(Cliff 96V1c)

Empty-handed gripping a hoe, go on foot astride a water-buffalo.

The Dharmakāya's subtly marvelous functioning, no-mind's subtly marvelous working.

終日走紅塵　失却自家珍

478. Shū|jitsu kō|jin-ni$_x$ washi(ri, ji|ka-no$_2$ chin-o$_3$ shik|kyaku-su$_1$.

A whole day bustling in the red dust
　Neglecting—rejecting—the treasure in your own house.

Your mind carried away by externals, to go on forgetting your own Buddha-nature.　["Red dust": The world with its cares.]

薫風自南來　殿閣生微涼

479. Kum|pū minami$_x$ yori kitari, den|kaku bi|ryō-o$_x$ shō(zu.

A fragrant breeze comes out of the south;
　The Dharma Hall produces a subtle coolness.

No-mind's fine state of mind. The sentence is to be taken as it is, as if the scene were right in front of you[!]. ["Fragrant": Summer.]

行到水窮處　坐看雲起時

480. Yui(te-wa ita(ru mizu-no kiwama(ru tokoro,
　　Za(shite-wa mi(ru kumo-no oko(ru toki.　[Wáng Wéi]

Going to get where the streams' source is
　Sitting to see when the clouds come up.

This speaks of the state of no-mind and of the use of no-mind.

詩向快人吟　酒逢知己飲

481. Shi-wa kai|jin-ni$_x$ muka(tte gin(ji, sake-wa chi|ki-ni$_x$ a(ute no(mu.　(Kidō 8)

The poem you face a quick man with—chant it;
　The wine you meet an intimate friend with—drink it!

Poems with a like-minded company, wine with true friends. Intimate friends, congenial spirits, are deeply familiar with how your spirit moves.

路逢達道人　不將語默對

482. Michi-ni tatsu|dō-no$_2$ hito-ni$_3$ a(waba$_1$, go|moku-o$_x$ mo(tte tai(se[zare.　(Mu 36K,V)

If you meet a man of the Way of complete insight on your way
　Don't give him words or silence in response.

When you meet a wise master, you must go beyond speech/silence.

達磨不會禪　夫子不知字

483. Daru|ma Zen-o$_x$ e(se[zu, Fū|shi ji-o$_x$ shi(ra[zu.

Bodhidharma hasn't infused himself with Zen;
　Confucius is ignorant of letters.

Bodhidharma is the embodiment of Zen, and Confucius that of literature; it's not a question of knowing or not knowing. "Fūshi": [Con-]fucius.

野火燒不盡　春風吹又生

484. Ya ka yake(domo tsu(ki[zu, shum|pū fu(ite mata shō(zu.　(Táng [Bái Jū-yì])

Wildfires burning don't finish them off;
　Spring breezes blow them alive again.

The weeds of passion kindled by the winds of this fleeting world; incessant birth-and-death.

金屑眼中翳　衣珠法上塵

485. Kin|setsu-wa gan|chū-no ei, e|ju-wa hō|jō-no chiri.　(Poison 5C; Realm 2)

A speck of gold in the eye shadows vision;
　Robes and beads are dust on the Dharma.

After marvelous enlightenment, even so-called blessings are actually defilements.

鐘聲來舊寺　月色下新池

486. Shō|sei kyū|ji-ni$_x$ kita(ri, ges|shoku shin|chi-ni$_x$ kuda(ru.　(Jōwa 7)

The bell's sound comes into the ancient monastery;
　The moonlight comes down into the fresh pool.

The present event as it is—an exquisite reflection of the truth.

長者長法身　短者短法身

487. Chō|ja-wa chō|hos|shin, tan|ja-wa tan|hos|shin.　(Zen 2)

The superior man is the Dharmakāya of superiority;
The inferior man is the Dharmakāya of inferiority.

Emancipated from separated individuality, the marvelous manifestations, *seriatim*, of the Dharmakāya.

陰陽不到處　一片好風光

488. In|yō fu|tō-no tokoro, ip|pen-no kō|fū|kō.　(Realm 5)

Where Yīn and Yáng don't reach: A bit of happy mental scenery.

The directness of enlightenment transcends the interacting cosmic forces; there the favorable fluctuating circumstances are beyond all expectation.

隨流認得性　無喜亦無憂

489. Nagare-ni$_x$ shitaga(tte sei-o$_x$ nin|toku-sureba, ki-mo$_x$ na(ku mata yū-mo$_x$ na(shi.
(Lamp 2; Rinzai 1XVIIId)

Going with the flow [of circumstances], realize [your own True] Nature
　And neither joy nor sorrow [will move you any more].

The wisdom of no-mind sees the truth with certainty, not fettered by joy and sorrow.

雲掩仲秋月　雨打上元燈

490. Kumo-wa chū|shū-no$_2$ tsuki-o$_3$ ō(i$_1$, ame-wa jō|gen-no$_2$ tomoshibi-o$_3$ u(tsu$_1$. (Realm 6)

Clouds hide the mid-autumn moon
　Rain pelts the festive lanterns.

A mass of clouds on the bright moon; pouring rain on myriads of lanterns. Clouds obscuring the moon and a storm on flowers are images [for life's uncertainties, its vexations and worries]. The "festival" is on the first of the first lunar month [February–March]—the "Feast of the Lanterns" in China, when paper lanterns are hung at every door—to enshrine the door. [The Midautumn Festival is on the full-moon day of the eighth lunar month.]

青山元不動　白雲自去來

491. Sei|zan moto fu|dō, haku|un onozuka(ra ko|rai.　　(Compendium)

The blue mountains never have moved;
　White clouds are always coming and going.

A mysterious natural scene. To forget your imperturbable original nature and go astray in clouds of vain distress.

TWELVE

一切聲是佛聲　一切色是佛色

492. Is|sai-no koe-wa ko(re Bus|shō, is|sai-no iro-wa ko(re Bus|shiki.　　(Cliff 79K)

Every sound is the Buddha's voice, every form the Buddha's appearance.

Seen with the penetrating insight of enlightenment, there is no experience that is not the complete revelation of the real Buddha.

一喝大地震動　一棒須彌粉碎

493. Ik|katsu dai|chi shin|dō(shi, ichi|bō Shu|mi fun|sai(su.　　(Comprehensive 5)

A shout: The solid ground quakes in shock;
　A stick—smashes Mount Sumeru to smithereens.

This saying praises Rinzai's "Gkhaught!!!!" and Tokusan's [blow with the] stick by pointing out their wonderful effects.

入息不居陰界　出息不涉萬緣

494. Nyus|soku on|kai-ni$_x$ o(ra[zu, shus|soku ban|en-ni$_x$ wata(ra[zu.　　(Kidō 1)

Breathing in, don't dwell on the realm of subjectivity;
　Breathing out, don't cling to reliance on objectivity.

The state of mind that doesn't lapse into the demons' cavern of discriminating thought within and doesn't wander astray into the outlying areas of the totality of multifarious things. The realm of subjectivity [literally, "concealing realm"] consists of: (1) The 5 *skandhas* [form (matter), feeling, thought, volition and consciousness]; (2) The 12 sense-mediums or entrances [the medium of the eye, of the ears, nose, tongue, body, mind; of form, sound, odor, taste, touch and thought]; (3) The 18 realms of sense [The eye, . . . , mind; form, . . . , thought; world of sight, . . . , world of consciousness]. [See the glossary of HTV. "Objectivity": Concern with the causal connections of the world's abounding entities, with all karma.]

去年貧未是貧　今年貧始是貧

495. Kyo|nen-no hin-wa ima(da ko(re hin-narazu, kon|nen-no hin-wa haji(mete ko(re hin.
　　　　　　　　　　　　　　　　　　　　　　　　　　　　　　　　　　(Kidō 1)

Last year's poverty was not yet real poverty;
　This year's poverty is, for the first time, poverty indeed.

Last year's enlightenment still smacked of enlightenment, but this year it lost that trace, becoming real enlightenment.

坐斷千聖路頭　打破群魔境界

496. Sen|shō-no₂ ro|tō-o₃ za|dan-shi₁, gum|ma-no₂ kyō|kai-o₃ da|ha-su₁.

Cut off the path of the thousands of sages
Smash the mind-state of the crowd of demons.

Crush both the Buddhas and the demons. This refers to the real state of enlightenment.

坐斷毘盧頂顙　曾不見有佛祖

497. Bi|ru|chō|nei-o ₓ za|dan-shite, kat(te Bus|so₃ a(ru-koto-o₂ mi[zu₁.

Cut off the top of Vairocana's head
And you'll stop seeing Buddhas and Patriarchs.

Thinking of no Buddhas or Patriarchs outside oneself, being on one's own, having shed all trappings —the non-dependent state of mind. It is the excellent Zen monks' true insight. [Vairocana's head: Delusions.]

大象不遊兔徑　大悟不拘小節

498. Dai|zō-wa to|kei-ni ₓ aso(ba[zu, tai|go-wa shō|setsu-ni ₓ kakawa(ra[zu.　(Song 56)

The great elephant doesn't frequent the hare's track
Supreme Enlightenment doesn't dwell on small matters.

The service [for all beings] of the great man of true enlightenment is not concerned with the petty affairs of conventional wisdom.

寒時寒殺闍梨　熱時熱殺闍梨

499. Kan|ji-wa ja|ri-o ₓ kan|sai-shi, netsu|ji-wa ja|ri-o ₓ nes|sai-su.　(Cliff 43K)

In times of cold, cold kills the ācārya;
In times of heat, heat kills the ācārya.

In cold times, cold penetrates through the whole body; in hot periods, heat penetrates through the whole body—they are the same. Ac(h)ārya [Sanskrit]: Oshō [Japanese—a monk, especially a teacher, a master of the precepts]. "Kills" is used for intensity. [For him it is *extremely* cold/hot.]

戰戰兢兢如臨　深淵如履薄氷

500. Sen|sen|kyō|kyō-to-shite shin|en-ni₃ nozo(mu-ga₂ goto(ku₁,
    Haku|hyō-o₃ fu(mu-ga₂ goto(shi₁.

On the alert, cautious—
As if looking into a deep chasm
As if walking on thin ice.

A simile for the intent self-control of a man of virtue who bravely dedicates his body to the great Way.

欲識佛性義理　當觀時節因緣

501. Bus|shō-no₃ gi|ri-o₄ shi(ran-to₂ hos(seba₁, masa-ni ji|setsu|in|nen-o ₓ kan(zu-beshi.

(Nirvāna)

If you want to understand the doctrine of Buddha-nature
You must contemplate the readiness of time.

If the readiness of time has not come, you cannot awaken to Buddha-nature. Be diligent in the practice of zazen!—and in time Great Enlightenment *will* come.

父有迷子之訣　子有打爺之拳

502. Chichi-ni mei|shi [no]₂ ketsu₃ a(ri₁, ko-ni ta|ya [no]₂ ken₃ a(ri₁.

The father has the cunning to deceive the son;
The son has the strength to beat the father.

Words of comment on Ōbaku and Rinzai ("father" and "son"). The father enlightens the son by misleading him. Enlightened, the son doesn't submit even to the father.

父母所生鼻孔　却在別人手裏

503. Fu|bo sho|shō-no bi|kū, kae(tte betsu|nin-no₂ shu|ri-ni₃ a(ri₁.　(Cliff 53Kn)

The nostrils of what was born of your father and mother
Are in the palm of another man's hand.

Don't you know they're your own nostrils (the Buddha-nature you've had from the beginning)? You surely don't think they're someone else's—do you? [In Chinese embryology, the nose is the starting point of the body's evolution.]

求美則不得美　不求美則美矣

504. Bi-o ₓ moto(mureba sunawa(chi bi-o ₓ e[zu, bi-o ₓ moto(me[zare(ba sunawa(chi bi [ ].

Seek the beautiful, and you won't get it;
Don't seek it, and—beauty!

Training in the Buddha's Way is just like this. Only when your way attains to being mindful in everyday life does it accord with the true Way.

爭如著衣喫飯　此外更無佛祖

505. Ikade-ka jaku|e₂ kip|pan-ni₃ shi(kan₁, kono hoka sara-ni Bus|so ₓ na(shi.

How?—things like donning robes and eating rice;
Besides this there are no Buddhas or Patriarchs.

The real Buddha is no place else; yourself, this moment, putting on clothes and eating food—this is it!

爲萬物之根源　作天地之太祖

506. Bam|butsu₂ no₃ kon|gen-to₄ na(ri₁, ten|chi₂ no₃ tai|so-to₄ na(ru₁.

Act as the root source of all things
Be the progenitor of the universe.

—like the true reality of suchness, the quintessence of all things. [Literally, "all": The ten thousand; "the universe": The heavens and the earth.]

文殊不識寒山　普賢不識拾得

507. Mon|ju Kan|zan-o_x shi(ra[zu, Fu|gen Jit|toku-o_x shi(ra[zu.　(Hán-shān, Introduction)

Mañjuśrī doesn't understand Hán-shān;
Samantabhadra doesn't understand Shí-dé.

Hán-shān is said to have been a reincarnation of Mañjuśrī [bodhisattva of wisdom] and Shí-dé of Samantabhadra [bodhisattva of compassion], but isn't not discriminatively knowing the most intimate?

聽鐘知有古寺　見烟覺有野村

508. Kane-o_x ki(ite ko|ji₃ a(ru-o₂ shi(ri₁, kemuri-o_x mi(te ya|son₃ a(ru-o₂ obo(u₁.

Hearing a bell, you know there's an ancient temple nearby;
Seeing smoke, you apprehend the presence of a country village.

Rising above everything to grasp the Great Matter. The usefulness of spiritual acuity.

處々眞處々眞　塵々盡本來人

509. Sho|sho shin sho|sho shin, jin|jin kotogoto(ku hon|rai-no hito.

Place after place is the right place,
　Place after place is the right place

Individual things are, each and all,
　The fundamental, original man.

Every place you come to clearly shows you the true Dharma, so there's nothing at all that's not your fundamental, original face [innate reality].

近則不離方寸　遠則十萬八千

510. Chika(ki [toki]-wa hō|sun-o_x hana(re[zu, tō(ki [toki]-wa jū|man|has|sen.

Near, not an inch away; far, a hundred and eight thousand.

Gain discernment, and THIS is close as your eyebrows—but go astray in ignorance [in the 108 passions and delusions], and it's a thousand, ten thousand miles away.

逐鹿者不見山　攫金者不見人

511. Shika-o_x o(u mono-wa yama-o_x mi[zu, kin-o_x tsuka(mu mono-wa hito-o_x mi[zu.
(Kidō 1)

Those who hunt the deer don't see the mountains
　Those who grasp for gold don't see men.

One-pointed samādhi, with everything else not registering; this illustrates that state with fortuitous fragments of it.

達磨不來東土　二祖不往西天

512. Daru|ma Tō|do-ni_x kita(ra[zu, Ni|so Sai|ten-ni_x yu(ka[zu.　(Zen 11)

Bodhidharma didn't come to the Eastern Land;
　The Second Patriarch didn't go to the Western Heaven.

[Respectively, China and India.] The meaning is that there is no coming or going of the true Dharma-kāya [Body of the Truth]. The Second Patriarch is Eka Daishi [Great Master Eka].

達磨不居少室　六祖不住曹溪

513. Daru|ma Shō|shitsu-ni$_x$ kyo(se[zu, Roku|so Sō|kei-ni$_x$ jū(se[zu.　(Kidō 5)

Bodhidharma never dwelt at Shōshitsu
The Sixth Patriarch never lived at Sōkei.

The real Bodhidharma and the real Sixth Patriarch are not their personal appearance, portraits or such like. The Dharmakāya is everywhere, always. Historically Bodhidharma lived at Shōrin-ji [-monastery] at Shōshitsu Peak and the Sixth Patriarch at Hōrin-ji by the stream called Sōkei.

雖與我同條生　不與我同條死

514. Ware$_3$ [to]$_2$ dō|jō-ni$_4$ shō(zu-to$_5$ iedo(mo$_1$, ware$_3$ [to]$_2$ dō|jō-ni$_4$ shi$_5$ [sezu]$_1$. (Cliff 51K)

Though it is with me, of the same lineage, that he is born,
It is not with me, of the same lineage, that he dies.

Even though the state of enlightenment is the same, the use it's put to, the way it's handled and so forth—are not the same.

FOURTEEN

515.

一二三四五六七　碧眼胡僧不知數

Ichi ni san shi go roku shichi,
Heki gan ko sō-mo sū-o$_x$ shi(ra[zu.　(Cliff 47V)

One, two, three, four, five, six, seven:

The blue-eyed barbarian-monk
Doesn't know how to count.

Eyes filled with it, ears filled with it, one living in the very midst of the fine and subtle Dharma, the wonderful Law, doesn't recognize it as such. The blue-eyed barbarian-monk is Bodhidharma.

516.

一口吸盡西江水　洛陽牡丹新吐蕊

Ik|ku-ni kyū|jin-su Sei|kō-no mizu,
Raku|yō-no bo|tan arata-ni zui-o$_x$ ha(ku.　(Realm 6)

At one swig
Drink the West River dry

In Luòyáng
The tree peonies bud again.

Untrammeled action after enlightenment—and, distracting thoughts swept clean away; entering the marvelous world of their dropping away is likened to what happens with the [white] tree peonies [in the ancient capital].

517.

一掇當機怒雷吼　驚起須彌藏北斗

Is|satsu ki-ni$_x$ ata(tte do|rai ho(yu,
Shu|mi-o$_x$ kyō|ki-shite Hoku|to-ni$_x$ kaku(ru.　(Compendium 20)

A goading rouses dynamism
At which raging thunder roars

Startling Mount Sumeru to rise up
And hide in the Big Dipper.

Since the dynamism and the goading are fundamentally an exchange of vows, the wonderful effect of the finest discernment is made to develop freely.

78

518.

一段風流玉琢成　一枝留得舊風流

Ichi|dan-no fū|ryū tama miga(ki na(su,
Is|shi todo(me e(tari kyū fū|ryū.　(Realm 5)

One last movement of the wind
And the gem is polished to perfection

A single branch retains, attains
The ancient movement of the wind.

Lines of admiration, the first for the white chrysanthemum, the second for the plum blossom. ["The movement of the wind": A metaphor for refinement.]

519.

一毫端現寶王刹　微塵裏轉大法輪

Ichi gō tan-ni hō|ō$_2$ setsu-o$_3$ gen-ji$_1$,
Mi jin ri-ni dai|hō$_2$ rin-o$_3$ ten-zu$_1$.　(Daie)

On a hair tip
Appears
The Treasure-King's shrine

In a dust mote
Turns
The Great Dharma Wheel.

This bespeaks the marvelously apt effect of spiritual penetration, the excellence of action after enlightenment. [Treasure-King: A title of the Buddha.]

520.

一片白雲橫谷口　幾多歸鳥夜迷巢

Ip|pen-no haku un kok|kō-ni$_x$ yokota(wari,
Iku|ta-no ki|chō-ka yoru su-ni$_x$ ma(you.　(Realm 5)

A single wisp of white cloud
Across the ravine's mouth

How many homing birds
Will the darkness mislead from their nests?

One seeking outside with his eye of wisdom unopened will probably end up without a place to come back to.

521.

一曲兩曲無人會　雨過夜塘秋水深

Ik|kyoku ryō|kyoku hito-no$_2$ e-suru$_3$ na(shi$_1$,
Ame su(gite ya|tō shū|sui fuka(shi.　(Cliff 37V)

One tune,
Another tune—
No one understands

After the downpour in the night
The autumn-clear water in the pools
Is intensely dark and deep.

It's not that these tunes are too refined to be generally appreciated. It's the mere fact that, full of autumn water, they [the pools] become perfectly still.

522.

一樹春風有兩般　南枝向暖北枝寒

Ichi|ju-no shum|pū ryō|han$_x$ a(ri,
Nan|shi-wa dan-ni$_x$ muka(i hoku|shi-wa kan.　(Realm 4)

A single tree gets the spring wind in two ways:

The south branches face the warmth
The north branches the cold.

Even the springtime beauty of one and the same tree manifests itself differently in its south branches
and its north branches. Diversity in sameness.

523.

一種是聲無限意　有堪聽與不堪聽

Is|shu ko(no koe kagi(ri$_x$ na(ki kokoro,
Ki(ku-ni$_3$ ta(yuru-to$_2$ ki(ku-ni$_6$ ta(e[zaru$_5$ [to]$_4$ a(ri$_1$.　(Realm 1)

A single kind of sound
[Gives rise to] an endless variety of feelings.

Some [sounds of that kind] we can bring ourselves to really hear;
Others we can't bear to listen to.

A composer's masterwork (that which is fundamental) has an implicit "taste," something totally irresis-
tible/unbearable.

524.

一粒粟中藏世界　半升鐺內煮山川

Ichi|ryū zoku|chū-ni se|kai-o$_x$ zō(shi,
Han|shō tō|nai-ni san|sen-o$_x$ ni(ru.　(Compendium 8)

In a single grain of millet
Conceal the world of time and space

Inside a two-pint vessel
Boil this land of mountains and rivers.

The freedom of action of enlightenment, the fine functioning when discriminative computations and
comparisons cease.

525.

一與山門作境致　二與後人作標榜

Hito(tsu-ni-wa sam|mon-no$_x$ tame-ni kyō|chi-to$_x$ na(shi,
Futatsu-ni-wa kō|jin-no$_x$ tame-ni hyō|bō-to$_x$ na(su.　(Rinzai 3II)

In the first place
To give the mountain gate a natural setting

Secondly
To give coming generations an emblem.

The reply of Rinzai Zenji while planting pines. We should consider the earnest dedication of the ancients
to the Dharma, and that we wear clothes of cloth woven by someone, eat food that is the fruit of labor
—! [Mountain gate: Main gate of the monastery.]

526.

一趯趯翻四大海　一拳拳倒須彌山

It|teki-ni teki|hon-su shi|dai|kai,
Ik|ken-ni ken|tō-su Shu|mi|san.　(Compendium 18)

With one kick
Kick up the four high seas

With one blow
Knock over Mount Sumeru.

Mighty actions with the freedom of enlightenment. Both the four oceans and Mount Sumeru become instruments to be played on.

527.

一重山盡又一重　話盡山雲海月情

Ichi|jū yama tsu(kite mata ichi|jū,
Kata(ri tsuku(su san|un kai|getsu-no jō.

Where one range of mountains ends
There's another range beyond

When talking to our hearts' content
There's the feeling of clouds in the mountains and the moon at sea.

Meaning, talk everything out, one thing right after the other, confide in each other to the bottom of our hearts [literally: *hara*, bellies]—a meeting of minds.

一陣西風吹雨過　夕陽總在海棠花

Ichi|jin-no sei|fū ame-o$_x$ fu(ite su(gu,
Seki|yō-wa su(bete kai|dō-no$_2$ hana-ni$_3$ a(ri$_1$.

528.

A single gust
Of west wind
Blows the rain clear away

The evening sun
Collects on
The cherry-apple blossoms.

—a poem that sings of a cherry crab tree in the rain—a fine scene occurring naturally. ["Collects on": Highlights.]

529.

三世諸佛不知有　狸奴白牯卻知有

San|ze sho|butsu a(ru-koto-o$_x$ shi(ra[zu,
Ri|nu byak|ko kae(tte a(ru-koto-o$_x$ shi(ru.　(Cliff 61Kc; Equanimity)

No Buddhas,
Past, present or future,
Know it exists

But the raccoon dog
And the white bull—
They know it exists.

The moment you say the "Bu" of Buddha, you defile your mind. If you recognize such distinctions as the higher people and the low or knowing and not knowing, you're deluded. [See #327.]

530.

三年辛苦已栽竹　一夜工夫又作梅

San|nen shin|ku-shite sude-ni take-o$_x$u(e,
Ichi|ya-no ku|fū mata ume-to$_x$na(ru.

> Three years of bitter suffering
> To finish
> Planting the bamboo
>
> One night of careful work
> More,
> And it turns out plum trees.

Putting the phrase another way: The fruit of three years of bitter suffering is that an undreamed-of great awakening is attained.

531.

三玄三要是何物　處處笙歌醉似泥

San|gen san|yō ko(re nani|mono-zo,
Sho|sho-no shō|ka yo(ute doro-ni$_x$ni(tari.　(Jōwa 3; Rinzai 1IX)

> The Three Mysteries and Three Essentials
> —What are they anyway?
>
> Everywhere, music to sing to
> Thoroughly plastered.

Never mind difficult things like Rinzai's Three Mysteries and Three Essentials—drink up and burst into song!

532.

三級浪高魚化龍　痴人猶戽夜塘水

San|kyū nami taka(u-shite uo ryū-to$_x$ka-su,
Chi|nin nao ku(mu ya|tō-no mizu.　(Cliff 7V)

> In the triple cascade's waves,
> The high-leaping fish
> Becomes a dragon
>
> But fools still
> Dip for it in the dark
> Pool [below].

Foolish fellows will go on transferring water to the end of time—after the carp that long ago became a dragon by ascending the threefold falls, called the [Dragon] Gate of Yǔ [founder of the Xià dynasty, 2205 B.C.].

533.

不見西湖林處士　一生受用只梅花

Mi[zu-ya Sei|ko-no Rin|sho|shi, is|shō-no ju|yō tada bai|ka.

> Don't you see?!:
> West Lake's Lín,
> The recluse
>
> —His life
> Devoted to taking in nothing but
> The plum blossoms.

The retired scholar Lín was Lín Hè Jīng. He spent his life gazing in admiration—appreciating—the plum blossoms. The subtle wonder of one-pointed samādhi. [The West Lake district was famous for culture.]

82

534.

九秋皓月當空照　一片白雲山上來

Kyū|shū-no kō|getsu tō|kū-ni tera(shi,
Ip|pen-no haku|un san|jō-yori kita(ru.

In autumn,
The glistening moon
Fills the sky with light

A drifting bit
Of white cloud
Comes over the mountains.

The state of mind of one free of busyness, greatly peaceful; a subtle image for the ultimate reality in its totality being here and now in *this* event as it is. Kyūshū: The nine(ty days of the three months) of autumn. [See #43.]

535.

五臺山上雲蒸飯　古佛堂前狗尿天

Go|dai|san jō kumo han-o$_x$ mu(shi,
Ko|butsu dō|zen inu ten-ni$_x$ nyō-su.

Clouds over Mount Wǔ-tái
—Steaming food

A dog before the ancient Buddha-hall
—Pissing heavenward.

The sight of the rising vapor forming clouds over Mount Wǔ-tái, the spectacle of the urinating dog in front of the hall. And, freedom in action after enlightenment.

536.

倒跨金毛獅子兒　無位眞人上五臺

Sakasama-ni kim|mō-no$_2$ shi|shiji-ni$_3$ mataga(tte$_1$,
Mu|i-no shin|nin Go|dai-ni$_x$ nobo(ru.

Backward astride
The golden-haired lion cub

The true man
With no rank climbs Wǔtái.

The dynamic action nothing-doing of the true man without rank, here likened to Mañjuśrī Bodhisattva. [Wǔtái is a mountain long sacred to Mañjuśrī. See Cliff 35K.]

537.

停車坐愛楓林晚　霜葉紅於二月花

Kuruma-o$_x$ todo(mete sozoro-ni ai(su fū|rin-no kure,
Sō|yō-wa ni|gatsu$_3$ [no]$_2$ hana-yori-mo$_4$ kurenai-nari$_1$.

Stopping the carriage I sit
Admiring the maple grove in the evening

The frosty leaves redder
Than spring flowers.

I can't help admiring the maple grove's red leaves, beautiful as the flowers in the second [lunar, in March and April] month (of spring). A subtle aspect of enlightenment as it is.

538. 兩岸猿聲啼不住　輕舟已過萬重山

Ryō|gan-no en|sei na(ite todomara[zu,
Kei|shū sude-ni su(gu ban|chō-no yama.　　(Táng [Dù Fǔ])

On both banks,
The sound of apes
Wailing without letup

The light boat
Has already left behind
Countless levels of the mountains.

Descending from the mountain citadel of the legendary White Emperor through rapids in the gorges, hearing the heartrending wails of the apes on both sides, the light boat shoots past like an arrow. And, the subtle flux of enlightenment to each present event as it is.

539. 到得歸來無別事　廬山烟雨浙江潮

Ita(ri e kae(ri kita(reba betsu|ji ₓ na(shi,
Ro|san-wa en|u Sek|ko-wa ushio.

Having gotten there and come back
It was no great thing:

Mount Lù's misty fine rain—
Zhé River's morning tide.

The meaning is that true, complete enlightenment is the same as not yet being enlightened. Complete enlightenment is misty fine rain and the river's morning tide, and to forget it is also misty fine rain and the river's morning tide [which Lù Mountain and the River Zhé are respectively famous for].

540. 勸君盡此一杯酒　西出陽關無故人

Kimi-ni ₓ susu(mu ko(no₂ ip|pai-no₃ sake-o₄ tsuku(se₁,
Nishi-no-kata yō|kan-o ₓ i(zureba ko|jin ₓ na(karan.　　[Wáng Wéi]

Come
Empty this
Cup of wine

West
Beyond the Yáng Barrier
There'll be no old friends.

A poem seeing someone off. "Come now, drink this cup of wine to the last drop, for henceforth you'll have no friends!"—meaning that you'll be interested in other ideas in other circumstances, in an endless succession of places. [The Yáng Barrier was a frontier checking station on a main artery (leading to the Silk Road) to the countries bordering western China.]

541. 十洲春盡花凋殘　珊瑚樹林日杲杲

Jis|shū haru tsu(kite hana chō|zan,
San|go ju|rin hi kō kō.　　(Cliff 70V)

In the isles of paradise, spring is over
The flowers withering away

On the forest of coral arms
The sun shines bright.

Even in Elysium, where a single spring lasts hundreds of years, spring comes to an end, but the sun shining makes the forest of never-withering coral bright. This expresses the state of mind of great enlightenment in terms of natural beauty.

542.

千峰萬峰不敢住　落花流水太茫茫

Sem|pō bam|pō ae(te todo(mara[zu,
Rak|ka ryū|sui hanaha(da bō|bō.　(Cliff 25V)

In the thousands of peaks
Myriads of peaks
Let yourself not dwell

Like falling flowers
Flowing water
Open, limitless.

When your whereabouts are unknown, at ease on the way, ceaselessly walking amid the scenery of insight, your subtle condition is as limitless as falling flowers and flowing water.

543.

千江有水千江月　萬里無雲萬里天

Sen kō mizu$_x$a(ri sen kō-no tsuki,
Ban ri kumo$_x$na(shi ban ri-no ten.

Thousands of rivers' waters
Thousands of river moons

Ten thousand miles without a cloud
Ten thousand miles of heaven.

When it's there, it's completely there; when not, it's completely non-existent [: Mu!, #14]. And, enlightenment's subtly fine point: This event here and now in its totality.

544.

南北東西歸去來　夜深同看千岩雪

Nam|boku|tō|zai kaeri nan iza,
Yoru fuka(u-shite ona(jiku mi(ru sen|gan-no yuki.　(Cliff 51V)

South, North, East, West,
Homeward let us go—

Deep in the night, seeing together
The snow on the thousand peaks.

Come now, let us all return. See the one who sees!—stop this pointless searching for good.

545.

去年貧有錐無地　今年貧無錐無地

Kyo|nen-no hin-wa sui$_x$a(tte chi$_x$na(ku,
Kon|nen-no hin-wa sui-mo$_x$na(ku chi-mo$_x$na(shi.　(Lamp 11)

Last year's poverty:
A gimlet point with no sticking place

This year's poverty:
Neither gimlet nor place.

Last year the sediment of enlightenment still remained; this year it's become nil. Shed, drop body, mind. [#409.]

只有文殊知此數　前三三與後三三

Tada Mon|ju-nomi$_x$ a(tte ko(no$_2$ sū-o$_3$ shi(ru$_1$,
Zen|san|san [to] go|san|san.　(Cliff 35K)

Only Mañjuśrī knows this number:
In front, threes and threes;
Behind, threes and threes.

[Or, in the context of the kōan:] The former, threes and threes; the latter, threes and threes—Mañjuśrī only knows how much this (apparently) low number is. Look with the insight of original wisdom! —and both the area in front and that behind are full of light and promise.

547.

在途中不離家舍　離家舍不在途中

To|chū-ni$_x$ a(tte ka|sha-o$_x$ hana(re[zu,
Ka|sha-o$_x$ hana(rete to|chū-ni$_x$ a(ra[zu.　(Rinzai 1VIII)

On the way without leaving home;
Having left home, not on the way.

"Home" is the fundamental Rank of the Real, and "on the way" is the wonderfully effective Rank of the Apparent. The true man's actions—*everything* he does—is beyond categorization—just as in the [Five] Ranks. [See ZD, p. 62–72.]

548.

堪對暮雲歸未合　遠山無限碧層層

Bo|un-no$_3$ kae(tte$_4$ ima(da$_5$ gas(sezaru-ni$_6$ tai-suru-ni$_2$ ta(etari$_1$,
En|zan kagi(ri$_x$ [naki] heki|sō|sō.　(Cliff 20V2)

What can compare
With clouds moving
Together
Toward evening?

—Far mountains
Without end,
Blue,
Range after range.

The beauty beyond description of tattered evening clouds in flight. The greenish layers of distant mountains seen in panorama. —This as it is is a vital revelation: It is a vital revelation of the true Buddha [the Dharmakāya]. [See also #351.]

549.

堪笑日月不到處　箇中別是一乾坤

Wara(u-ni$_x$ ta(etari jitsu|getsu fu|tō-no tokoro,
Ko(no uchi betsu-ni ko(re ichi|ken|kon.　(Comprehensive 21)

Keep smiling
Where sun and moon do not reach

And whether we're together or apart
It's all one universe.

The places where sun and moon don't reach are gathering places specially set aside—are they at variance with everything being straightforward and apparent, on display, obvious?

550.

壺中自有佳山水　終不重尋五老峰

Ko|chū onozuka(ra ka|san|sui$_x$[ari],
Tsui-ni kasa(nete Go|rō|hō-o$_x$ tazu(ne[zu.

Within the pot
There naturally are beautiful mountains and rivers

It's of the utmost importance
To search for Wǔlǎo Peak.

Already aware of the scenic splendors of another universe, there's no need at all to visit the sights on your way to another place. Wǔlǎo is the name of a peak of Mount Lù.

551.

大地撮來粟米粒　一毫頭上現乾坤

Dai|ji satsu-shi kita(ru-ni zoku|bei|ryū,
Ichi|gō tō|jō-ni ken|kon-o$_x$ gen(zu.　　(Comprehensive 29)

From the great earth
Pinch up a rice-grain

On a thin hair tip
Reveal the universe!

Fundamental dynamism. Great insight in subtle action. The freedom that goes beyond size and distance data.

552.

如今抛擲西湖裏　下載清風付與誰

Nyo|kon hō|teki-su Sei|ko-no uchi,
A|sai-no sei|fū tare-ni-ka$_x$ fu|yo-sen.　　(Cliff 45V)

Now I've thrown it out
Into West Lake

To whom can I give
The cool breeze along the surface?

The troublesome burden [the self] thrown into the middle of the lake, there's no way to express [no other to give] the delight of the unburdened breath of fresh air.

553.

妙峰孤頂難人到　只看白雲飛又歸

Myō|bu Ko|chō hito$_2$ ita(ri$_3$ gata(shi$_1$,
Tada mi(ru haku|un-no to(nde mata kae(ru-koto-o.　　(Realm 5:6V)

The Isolated Summit of Wonder Peak
Is hard for a man to reach

But see the white clouds
Flying there and coming back again.

This summit [metaphor for the realization that beings and Buddhas are not two] of Wonder Peak [Mt. Sumeru, the central mountain of the universe] is the place where [the young pilgrim] Sudhana [in the Wreath Sutra] calls on the almsman Tokuun [Sagaramegha]. Unable to get to the directness of the fundamental, still one can simply keep quiet, free of care.

安禪不必須山水　滅却心頭火自涼

An|zen-wa kanara(zu-shimo san|sui-o$_x$ mochi(i[zu,
Shin|tō-o$_x$ mek|kyaku-sureba hi-mo onozuka(ra suzu(shi.　(Cliff 43Kc)

> Peaceful Zen
> Has no need of mountains and waters

> The mind extinguished,
> Even fire is cool.

Zazen shouldn't be limited to the quiet mountains. There is unshakeable peace of mind in any place where the mind is freed of thoughts. "Even when a tea dipper is dipped into something cold as a cold hell or hot as a hot hell, it has no pain at all, because it has no-mind."—Sen no Rikyu [the Tea Master]. The marvelous enlightenment that goes beyond heat and cold. [Extinguished: Like a candle.]

555.

寒松一色千年別　野老拈花萬國春

Kan|shō is|shiki sen|nen betsu-nari,
Ya|rō hana-o$_x$ nen(zu ban|koku-no haru.　(Rinzai 3XIII)

> The winter pine
> Evergreen
> [Un]changed for thousands of years

> The country gaffer
> Holds up a flower
> And it's spring in all lands.

The splendor of the ancient pines, their color unchanging; and, when the old villager enjoys a flower, the tranquillity of spring the world over.

556.

寒梅的的西來意　一片西飛一片東

Kam|bai teki|teki sai|rai i,
Ip|pen-wa nishi-ni to(bi ip|pen-wa higashi.

> The winter plum clearly details
> The meaning of the coming from the West

> One petal drifting westward
> Another eastward.

A single branch of winter plum blossoms. When they're scattered toward the West, they're also scattered toward the East. The clear intention [of Bodhidharma] in coming from the West is one, though its applications may naturally be two or three.

557.

寒雲籠雪夕陽重　山月照梅夜色清

Kan|un yuki-o$_x$ ko(mete seki|yō omo(ku,
San|getsu ume-o$_x$ tera(shite ya|shoku kiyo(shi.　(Realm 2)

> Wintry clouds full of snow
> The evening sun heavy

> The mountain moon shines on the plum
> The night's beauty clear.

The wintry clouds with no mind to, the mountain moon with no intention—just holding, just shining —a very deep and subtle implication. Subtle scenery symbolic of the state of the true man.

558.

山僧活計茶三畝　漁夫生涯竹一竿

San|sō-ga kak|kei cha sam|po,
Gyo|fu-no shō|gai take ik|kan.

This mountain monk's occupation
Is with three *mŏ* of tea

The fisherman's means of livelihood
Is one bamboo pole.

Each of us has his own unique state of mind and situation. And, the real state of the man of the Way, living simply and in clarity. [This mountain monk: "I" (self-deprecatory); 3 *mŏ* is a little less land than ½ acre.]

559.

巨靈擡手無多子　分破華山千萬重

Kyo|rei te-o $_x$ mota(guru-ni ta|su $_x$ na(shi,
Bum|pa-su Ka|zan-no sen|ban|chō.　　(Cliff 32V; Mu 3V)

Kyorei raised his hand
With no great effort

And split Mount Ka:
Thousands, tens of thousands of heavy layers!

In the same way as the [Chinese] god Kyorei just moved his hand a bit to cleave the great Ka Mountain in two, the apt dynamism after enlightenment, the skill and fitness of action, is infinite.

560.

常憶江南三月裏　鷓鴣啼處百花香

Tokoshie-ni omo(u Kō|nan san|gatsu-no uchi,
Sha|ko na(ku tokoro hyak|ka kamba(shi.　　(Mu 24K; Realm 5:11Vn [Dù Fǔ])

I'm always thinking
Of the region south of the River
In May

The partridge
Calling
Amid hundreds of flowers' fragrance.

The beauty of the luminosity and color—the spring scenery—in the country south of the Yángzǐ. The finely subtle state of true awareness of the here-and-now as it is.

561.

年年歲歲花相似　歲歲年年人不同

Nen|nen sai|sai hana ai ni(tari,
Sai|sai nen|nen hito onaji(kara[zu.　　(Táng [Bái Jū-yì])

Year by year
Year after year
The flowers appear alike

Year after year
Year by year
Men are not the same.

Every year, the flowers bloom, looking lovely, but the ever-changing human generations are pathetically short-lived.

562.

庭前有月松無影　欄外無風竹有聲

Tei|zen-ni tsuki_x a(ri matsu-ni kage_x na(ku,
Ran|gai kaze_x na(u-shite take-ni koe_x a(ri.

In the courtyard
Moon[light]—
[But] the pine has no shadow

Beyond the fence
No wind—
[But] in the bamboo there's sound.

Completely become, be one with, seeing the moon, the moon *only*—with hearing sound, *mere* sound. The samādhi of this completely becoming, being one with.

563.

徐行踏斷流水聲　縱觀寫出飛禽跡

Omomuro-ni yu(ite tō dan-su ryū sui-no koe,
Hoshiimama-ni mi(te utsu(shi ida(su hi kin-no ato.　　(Cliff 6V)

Quietly moving along
You "wade" away
The flowing waters' sound

Widely gazing
You "take"
The flying birds' tracks.

Stop the sound of the flowing water; retain the image of the birds' tracks. The real state of wondrous enlightenment: Becoming the water completely, becoming the birds completely.

564.

愁人莫向愁人説　説向愁人愁殺人

Shū|jin shū|jin-ni₃ muka(tte₂ to(ku-koto₄ naka(re₁,
Shū|jin-ni_x setsu|kō-sureba hito-o_x shū|satsu-su.　　(Cliff 40Vn)

Don't speak sadness to a sad man

If you tell it to a sad man
It will make him terribly sad.

One who has had bitter experience well understands words of sorrow (becomes full of another's grief) —but, if he's not a kindred spirit with profound personal experience, he will miss the true meaning.

565.

數片白雲籠古寺　一條綠水繞青山

Sū|hen-no haku|un ko|ji-o_x ko(me,
Ichi|jō-no ryoku|sui sei|zan-o_x megu(ru.　　(Comprehensive 2)

Many slips of white cloud
Have caught the ancient temple like a net

A single stream of emerald water
Surrounds the blue mountains.

A subtle image that reveals the fundamental; there is absolutely nothing else worthy of wonder.

566.

昨夜金烏飛入海　曉天依舊一輪紅

Saku ya kin u to(nde umi-ni$_x$ i(ri,
Gyō ten furu(ki-ni$_x$ yo(tte ichi rin kurenai-nari.　(Ox 9)

Yesterday evening
The Golden Crow
Flew into the sea

This morning dawn
Comes with the owl-old same
Disk of red.

When everything is exhausted and shaken off, glorious light fills the world. The Golden Crow is the sun.

567.

春宵一刻價千金　花有清香月有陰

Shun|shō ik|koku atai sen|kin,
Hana-ni sei|kō$_x$ a(ri tsuki-ni kage$_x$ a(ri.

A spring evening's single half hour
Is worth a thousand gold pieces

—The flowers have clear fragrances
The moon casts shadows.

Immeasurable in money is the pleasure of a spring night: The fragrance of the flowers, the elegance of the moon, the richness of life.

568.

春江潮水連海平　海上明月共潮生

Shun|kō-no chō|sui umi-ni$_x$ tsura(natte taira(ka-ni,
Kai|jō-no mei|getsu ushio-to$_x$ tomo-ni shō-zu.　(Realm 1)

In spring
The river's tide
Goes evenly on out to sea

On the sea
The bright moon
Rises along with the morning tide.

A really shining, auspicious scene. Take it in to the limit of your senses, eyes full of it, ears full of it —and there is nothing beyond it.

569.

最愛江南三月後　青山綠樹囀黃鸝

Motto(mo ai-su Kō|nan san|gatsu-no nochi,
Sei|zan ryoku|ju-ni kō|ri-o$_x$ ten(zu.

Most loved,
The region south of the river
At the end of May

The blue mountains,
The green trees
Melodious with yellow orioles.

The natural beauty of late spring and the sentiment it evokes—and, a subtle image for insight into this present event as it is.

月落烏啼霜滿天　江楓漁火對愁眠

Tsuki o(chi karasu na(ite shimo ten-ni~x~mi(tsu
Kō fū-no gyo ka shū|min-ni~x~tai-su.　(Tang [Zhāng Jì])

When the moon has set
　Crows caw
　　And frost fills the heavens

On the river, against the maples
　Fishing fires
　　—Disturb nostalgic sleep.

[Gūsū city
　Is beyond
　　The Hán-shān-sì

Whose midnight bell
　Sounds
　　—Reaching our pilgrim boat.]

A scene on the riverbank when the moon is down on an autumn night, the cold intense—a feeling of being quiet and apart. The subtle taste of true insight into the present fleeting moment as it really is. [The title of this poem is "A Night Moored at Maple Bridge". Gūsū is now Sūzhōu. Hán-shān-sì: Cold Mountain Monastery.]

月從雪後皆奇夜　天到梅邊有別春

Tsuki-wa setsu|go~x~[yori] mina ki|ya,
Ten-wa bai|hen-ni~x~ita(tte bes|shun~x~a(ri.

The moon coming after a snow
　—An altogether marvelous night

The weather in the plum's ambience
　Is a separate spring.

Viewing the moon after a snow is delightful; the weather is even more spring-like with the blooming of the plum.

東風吹散梅梢雪　一夜挽回天下春

Tō|fū fu(ki san(zu bai|shō-no yuki,
Ichi|ya-ni ban|kai-su ten|ka-no haru.

The east wind blows away
　The snow on the plum twigs

That same night brings spring again
　Everywhere under heaven.

Verses on the first day of spring. When the east wind sweeps the snow off the plum twigs, spring comes that same night.

573.

梅邊殘月無疎影　竹裏清風有落花

Bai|hen-no zan|getsu so|ei_x[naku].
Chiku|ri-no sei|fū rak|ka_x[ari].　(Realm 1)

Around the plum trees
　The pale moon
　　Casts no scattered shadows

Within the bamboo
　The fresh breeze
　　Bears along fallen blossoms.

The light of the moon at dawn is so faint the plum trees have no shadows, and the pure breeze full of falling flowers soughs in the bamboo. A subtle taste of enlightenment actualized, as it is.

574.

榔㮧横擔不顧人　直入千峰萬峰去

Shitsu|ritsu ō-ni nina(tte hito-o_x kaeri(mi[zu,
Jiki-ni sem|pō|mam|pō-ni_x i(ri sa(ru.　(Cliff 25K)

Shouldering his ashen staff
　Not turning to look at people

He heads right in to the thousands,
　Myriads of peaks—gone.

The ashen staff is given to old or feeble sangha members. For the sake of saving all beings, he's forgotten how to come to a standstill in one place.

575.

歸家擔子兩頭脱　柴自青分火自紅

Ie-ni_x kae(tte tan|su ryō|tō das(su,
Shiba-wa onozuka(ra ao(ku [ ] hi-wa onozuka(ra kurenai-nari.

Back home, with both ends of the load put down
　The logs are a natural dun color, the fire naturally red.

Returning to your fundamental, original home, throw off all your painful distressing delusions, and willows are green, flowers red, after all.

576.

毘婆尸佛早留心　直到如今不得妙

Bi|ba|shi|butsu haya(ku shin-o_x todo(muru-mo,
Jiki-ni nyo|kon-ni_x ita(tte myō-o_x e[zu.　(Mu 22C)

Though Vipaśyin Buddha
　Has been mindful for ages

So far he hasn't got at
　The profound and subtle essence.

Vipaśyin Buddha is the Buddha who lived before the "empty" kalpa [when all is in a state of utter dissolution]. He had set his mind on the Way since of old, but got nothing whatever. To live *without* gaining the essence is the ultimate essence indeed!

577.   水自竹邊流出冷　風從花裏過來香

Mizu-wa chiku|hen ₓ[yori] ryū shutsu-shite hiyaya(ka-ni,
Kaze-wa ka|ri ₓ[yori] su(gi kita(tte kamba(shi.   (Zen 8)

Water
Bordering bamboo
Flows draining from them
Cold

Breezes
Through flowers
Come from among them
Fragrant.

The subtle taste of the fundamental quality of this fleeting moment. Those who haven't passed through hardship can't taste this.

578.   江上晚來堪畫處　漁人披得一蓑歸

Kō|jō ban|rai ega(ku-ni ₓ ta(etaru tokoro,
Gyo|jin is|sa-o₃ hi-shi₁ e(te₂ kae(ru.

On the river
Evening comes
—A scene worth painting

Now the fisherman's
Able to throw on
His straw cope and go home.

A fine scene on the river. The subtle import of the actual fact of the present event as it is in all its suchness.

579.   江國春風吹不起　鷓鴣啼在深花裏

Kō|koku-no shum|pū fu(ki ta(ta[zu,
Sha|ko-wa na(ite shin|ka-no₂ ura-ni₃ a(ri₁.   (Cliff 7V)

In the river country
The spring wind's
Blowing
Is motionless

The partridge
Calling
—Is somewhere
Deep in the flowers.

The superb spring landscape in the river country. And, a subtly fine image for enlightenment to this event here and now, as it is. [Followed by #532.]

580.   泉州白家酒三盞　喫了猶言未沾脣

Sen|shū Hak|ke sake san san,
Kis(shi owa(tte nao i(u ima(da kuchibiru-o ₓ uruo(sazu-to.   (Mu 10K)

Three cups of wine from the House of Bái in Quán Province—
You've finished them and still you say you've yet to wet your lips!

Though he drinks three big cups of pure Cabernet Sauvignon, he's left with no feeling of having done so. Not to know is the most intimate.

94

581.

湘潭雲盡暮山出　巴蜀雪消春水來

Shō|tan kumo tsu(kite bo|san i(de,
Ha|shoku yuki ki(ete shun|sui kita(ru.　(Realm 4)

The Xiāng's pools' clouds dispersed
Evening-sunlit mountains appear

The Sìchuān snows melting
Spring freshets come forth.

When the discrimination of delusion and enlightenment, of commoner and sage, completely comes to
nothing, the subtly marvelous working of no-mind has begun.

582.

溪聲便是廣長舌　山色豈非清淨身

Kei sei sunawa(chi ko(re kō chō zetsu,
San shoku ani shō|jō|shin-ni ₓ ara[zaran-ya.　[Sū Dōng-pō]

The mountain stream's sound
Has got to be the broad, long tongue

The mountains' beauty—
How could it not be that of the shining pure body?

The sound of the mountain stream is *this* Tathāgata's preaching, the appearance of the mountains is
this Buddha's marvelously apparent body. [Broad, long tongue: Eloquence.]

583.

無一物中無盡藏　有花有月有樓臺

Mu|ichi|motsu chū mu|jin|zō,
Hana ₓ a(ri tsuki ₓ a(ri rō|dai ₓ a(ri.

There is not one thing
—And within this,
Inexhaustibility:

There are flowers
There is the moon
There is the pagoda.

Once you—your ego—undergo combustion, Look!—penetrate to the true source of the universe, and
see that there is no such thing as your self. Then the things you see, the things you hear, all are the
light.

584.

無始劫來生死本　痴人喚作本來人

Mu|shi gō|rai shō|ji-no moto,
Chi|nin-wa yo(nde hon|rai-no₂ hito-to₃ na(su₁.　(Cliff 99Kc; Mu 12V)

Of beginningless ages
Of birth-and-death
The root:

Fools take it
For the fundamental, essential
Self.

A verse of Chōsa Zenji. To labor under the delusion that the discriminating mind, the root cause of the
onflowing vicious circle of births and deaths, *is* your Buddha-nature.

585. 猿抱子歸青嶂後　鳥啣花落碧岩前

Saru-wa ko-o_x ida(ite sei|shō-no₂ shirie-ni₃ kae(ri₁,
Tori-wa hana-o_x fuku(nde heki|gan-no₂ mae-ni₃ o(tsu₁.

(Compendium 5; Lamp 15; Realm 2)

> The apes cradle fruit
> As they return to the far side
> Of the gray-green peaks
>
> A bird holds a flower in its beak,
> Then lets it fall
> Before the blue rock.

The marvelous appearance of the fundamental reality here and now. To the question, "What is the state of Kassan [*and* the mountain he was named for]?"—Kassan's answer was this verse.

586. 玉殿深沈夜將半　斷猿空叫月明中

Gyoku|den shin|chin-to-shite yoru masa-ni nakaba-naran-to-su,
Dan|en muna(shiku sake(bu getsu|mei-no uchi.

> A gem of a palace
> Intensely still
> —Near midnight
>
> Lacerating
> An ape's empty wailing
> In the moonlight.

Nirvāna is as the deep stillness of a splendid palace in the dead of night, the gut-rending pathetic cry of a gibbon wailing under the cold, clear moon. The subtle state of desolate courage in the splendid isolation of special excellence.

587. 王令已行徧天下　將軍塞外絕烟塵

Ō|rei sude-ni okona(warete ten|ka-ni_x ama(neshi,
Shō|gun sai|gai-ni en|jin-o_x zes(su.　(Rinzai 1X)

> The sovereign's authority
> Already prevails
> Everywhere under heaven
>
> The commanding general
> Beyond the frontier
> Has laid the smoke and dust [of battle].

The Emperor's mandates are operative throughout the empire, well governed even beyond the border. Peace of mind.

588. 珊瑚枕上兩行淚　半是思君半恨君

San|go chin|jō ryō|kō-no nanda,
Nakaba-wa ko(re kimi-o_x omo(i nakaba-wa kimi-o_x ura(mu.　(Realm 4)

> On the coral pillow
> Two streams of tears:
>
> Half longing for you
> Half hating you.

A beauty in her bedchamber chants a litany of malice. The bitter [suffering] tears of this fixed [delusive] desire may turn into Bodhi [enlightenment].

96

589.

現成一段西來意　一片西飛一片東

Gen|jō ichi|dan sai|rai-no i,
Ip|pen-wa nishi-ni to(bi ip|pen-wa higashi.　(Jōwa 9)

Revealed all the more:
The meaning of the coming out of the West

—In one petal flying westward
Another eastward.

Even the scattering of blossoms both eastward and westward is, now, before your eyes, a manifestation
of the meaning (the Buddha-dharma) of the coming [of Bodhidharma] from the West.

590.

白雲盡處是青山　行人更在青山外

Haku|un tsu(kuru tokoro ko(re sei|zan,
Kō|jin-wa sara-ni sei|zan-no$_2$ hoka-ni$_3$ a(ri$_1$.　(Jōwa 1)

When the white clouds are gone
There are the blue mountains

Travelers, though
Go everyplace but the blue mountains.

This has to be called a subtle image for insight realized as it is.

591.

百尺竿頭進一歩　十方刹土現全身

Hyaku|shaku kan|tō-ni ip|po-o$_x$ susu(me,
Jip|pō setsu|do-ni zen|shin-o$_x$ gen(zu.　(Mu 46K)

Step off the top of the hundred-foot pole
And manifest your whole being throughout the world.

When you've thoroughly mastered upward advancement, turning downward, going one step further,
appearing where you've gotten to, enlighten all beings.

592.

相送當門有脩竹　爲君葉葉起清風

Ai oku(tte mon-ni$_x$ ata(reba shū|chiku$_x$ [ari],
Kimi-ga$_x$ ta(me-ni yō yō sei|fū-o$_x$ oko(su.　(Kidō 7)

To see you off
There's a setting of bamboo at the gate

For your sake
Each leaf rustles in the cool breeze.

Hospitality overflowing with refined and affectionate friendship. The depth of feeling of a noble man
expressed in the purity of his way of saying farewell.

593. 　　石女舞成長壽曲　木人唱起太平歌　　97

Seki|jo ma(i-o na(su chō|ju-no kyoku,
Moku|jin tona(e oko(su tai|hei-no uta.　(Realm 4)

The stone woman dances
To the tune "Longevity"

The wooden man chants
The poem "Lasting Peace".

Effective words on the fundamental. The mysterious function of what doesn't happen, which is beyond emotional and intellectual discernment.

594. 　　秋天曠野行人絶　馬首東來知是誰

Shū|ten kō|ya kō|jin ta(yu,
Ba|shu tō|rai-su shi(nnu ko(re ta-zo.　(Poison 23C; Táng [Wáng Chāng-líng])

Autumn's clear sky
On the vast plain—
No travelers at all

On a horse
Coming East
You *know*—it's—who?

The autumn scene of hushed discontent in the wilderness beyond the frontier. Almost imperceptibly in the distance, something moving: A lone horseman at the edge of this prairie devoid of travelers. When all is exhausted, all avenues cut off, the spring of better times returns of itself.

595. 　　空山白日蘿窓下　聽罷松風午睡濃

Kū zan haku jitsu ra|sō-no moto,
Shō|fū-o$_3$ ki(ki$_1$ ya(nde$_2$ go|sui komayaka-nari.　[Jakushitsu]

Empty mountains
And bright sun
Through the ivied window

Having listened
To the wind in the pines,
The nap is deep.

A metaphor for the quiet, free and open state of mind of the calm man of the Way with no doings. ["Empty": Unpeopled.]

596. 　　竹影掃堦塵不動　月穿潭底水無痕

Chiku|ei kai-o$_x$ hara(tte chiri dō(ze[zu,
Tsuki tan|tei-o$_x$ uga(tte mizu-ni ato$_x$ na(shi.　(Realm 5: 23Vn)

The bamboos' shadows
Sweep the stairs
—The dust does not move

The moonlight pierces
To the pool's bottom
—The water is unmarked.

Everything you do forgetting your self is entirely spotless, impeccable. Light and darkness paired bespeak the marvelous effect of non-doing.

597.

終日行而未曾行　終日説而未曾説

Shūjitsu gyō(ji[te] ima(da kat(te gyō(zezu,
Shūjitsu to(i[te] ima(da kat(te to(kazu.　(Cliff 16I)

A whole day in action without having acted
A whole day of teaching without having taught.

Meaning, penetrating, constant practice-and-teaching without contrivance, selfless. A man of old [Sōsan Ganchi Zenji] said, "The way of words is cut" [#163]—that is, *all* words; "where the mind moves is destroyed"—that is, *all* acts.

598.

良藥苦口利於病　忠言逆耳利於行

Ryō|yaku kuchi-ni$_x$ niga(u-shite yamai$_3$ [ni]$_2$ ri-ari$_1$,
Chū|gen mimi-ni$_x$ sakara(e-domo okonai$_3$ [ni]$_2$ ri-ari$_1$.　[Confucius]

Good medicine
Though bitter in the mouth
Eases disease

Frank advice
Though grating to the ear
Improves conduct.

The meaning of this phrase is clear—and yet people dislike the necessary bitterness of effective medicine, and resent the unpleasantness of sincere advice.

599.

花開不假栽培力　自有春風管對伊

Hana-no hira(ku-koto-wa, sai|bai-no$_2$ chikara-o$_3$ ka(ra[zu$_1$,
Onozuka(ra shum|pū-no$_2$ kare-o$_4$ kan|tai-suru$_3$ a(ri$_1$.　(Realm 1)

Flowers don't bloom
With the energy of planting and earthing them up

They naturally have the spring
Breezes to regulate and respond to them.

The flowers are not made to blossom by human effort—you should know that it's due to a tremendous natural power: The energy of the spring breezes.

600.

芭蕉葉上愁雨聲　只是時人聽斷腸

Ba|shō yō jō-ni shū|u-no koe,
Tada ko(re toki-no hito kii(te dan|chō.

The sound of depressing rain
On the plantain leaves—

Just listening to this now,
I'm heartbroken.

Grasses and trees fundamentally have no such mind—the being depressed to distraction is in the mind of the one who hears. [Bashō is also the name of the banana "tree"—of the same genus—from which the Japanese poet Bashō Matsuō took his pen-name. "Heartbroken": Literally, with lacerated bowels.]

荷葉團團團似鏡　菱角尖尖尖似錐

Ka|yō dan dan-to-shite kagami₃ yo(ri-mo₂ madoka-nari₁,
Ryō|kaku sen sen-to-shite kiri₃ yo(ri-mo₂ surudo(shi₁.　(Daie; Compendium 5)

The lotus leaves:
Round, round—
Round as mirrors

The water-chestnut horns:
Sharp, sharp—
Sharp as gimlets!

The roundness of the leaves of the lotus, the sharpness of the horns of water-chestnuts—subtle images for enlightenment to the present event as it is.

602.

落花有意隨流水　流水無情送落花

Rak|ka i ₓ a(tte ryū|sui-ni ₓ shitaga(i,
Ryū|sui jō ₓ na(ushite rak|ka-o ₓ oku(ru.　(Realm 5)

The fallen flower
Goes willingly
With the flowing water

The flowing water,
Unmoved,
Carries the fallen flower away.

The fallen flower going willingly is, as it is, unmoved; the flowing water's being unmoved is, as it is, true feeling. And, the subtle taste of enlightenment to the present event as it is.

603.

路逢劍客須呈劍　不是詩人莫獻詩

Michi-ni ken|kaku-ni ₓ a(waba subekara(ku ken-o ₓ tei-subeshi,
Ko(re₂ shi|jin-ni₃ ara[zu(mba₁ shi-o₃ ken(zuru-koto₂ naka(re₁.　(Cliff 38Kc; Rinzai 3XIX)

If you meet a swordsman on the road
You must offer him [a taste of] your sword

Unless he's a poet
You mustn't offer him a poem.

Seeing someone, expounding the Dharma, if he's a true friend [of the Dharma] of like mind, it's OK to talk freely—but with an unfeeling honorable visitor, be reserved!

604.

通玄不是人間世　滿目青山何處尋

Tsū|gon-wa ko(re₂ nin|gen|se ni₃ [arazu]₁,
Mam|moku-no sei|zan izu(re-no tokoro-ni-ka tazu(nen.　(Compendium 18)

The Penetralia of Mystery
Are not of this human life

As far as the eye can see,
Blue mountains—where to seek?

In Taoism, the peak summits called the Penetralia of Mystery are said not to be in the human world —but then where could that kind of peak be?

605.

雪後始知松柏操　事難方見大夫心

Setsu go haji(mete shi(ru shō|haku-no misao,
Koto kato(u-shite masa-ni mi(ru jō|bu-no shin.　(Realm 5: 11Kn)

After a snow
You realize anew
The constancy of pine and cedar

When the going gets rough
You clearly feel
Firmness of spirit.

When he meets with life's trials, you comprehend for the first time the true worth of an able man. ["Constancy": Being evergreen.]

606.

雲在嶺頭閑不徹　水流磵下大忙生

Kumo-wa rei|tō-ni $_x$ a(tte kan fu|tetsu,
Mizu-wa kan|ka-o $_x$ naga(rete tai|bō|sei.　(Realm 4)

Clouds dwell
On the mountain peak
Serene

Water runs down
Through the rocks,
Full of rushing life.

The serenity is that of mighty nirvāna, and full, rushing life stands for being extremely busy. The subtle sense of enlightenment to this present event as it is.

607.

雲開月色家家白　春過山花處處紅

Kumo hira(kete ges|shoku ya|ya shiro(ku,
Haru su(gite san|ka sho|sho kurenai-nari.

When the clouds part
There's moonlight in every home
White

When spring passes
There're autumn leaves everywhere
Crimson.

A subtle image for insight into the present event as it is. [Autumn leaves: Literally, "mountain flowers".]

608. 　青山綠水元依舊　明月清風共一家　

Sei|zan ryoku|sui moto furu(ki-ni_x yoru,
Mei|getsu sei|fū tomo-ni ik|ka.　(Compendium 20)

> The blue mountains
> And green water
> Are as of old

> And the bright moon,
> The clear breeze—
> They're all one family.

From the enlightened point of view, the grayish-blue mountains and aquamarine waters are as they
have always been, and the glistening moon and pure breeze are also the same as they were in antiquity.
The mystery is above and beyond that.

609. 　風吹不動天邊月　雪壓難摧澗底松

Kaze fu(ke-domo dō(ze[zu tem|pen-no tsuki,
Yuki o(se-domo kuda(ke_x gata(shi kan|tei-no matsu.　(Comprehensive 16)

> The wind, no matter how it blows
> Doesn't move
> The moon in the sky.

> The snow, no matter how heavily it presses down
> Doesn't break down
> The pine over the mountain torrent.

Apt metaphors, beautifully expressed, for the Buddha-nature, unborn, indestructible, this real, present
body of each and all—in all its completeness.

610. 　風吹柳絮毛毬走　雨打梨花蛺蝶飛

Kaze ryū|jo-o_x fu(keba mō|kyū hashi(ri,
Ame ri|ka-o_x u(teba kyō|chō to(bu.　(Daie)

> When the wind blows
> Over the willow catkins,
> Their fluff balls roll away [on the ground]

> When rain pelts
> The pear blossoms,
> Their petals fly like swallowtails.

The willow flowers falling, the pear-tree flowers flying—scenes with subtle implications for enlighten-
ment to the present event as it is.

611. 　風吹碧落浮雲盡　月上青山玉一團

Kaze heki|raku-o_x fu(ite fu|un tsu(ki,
Tsuki sei|zan-ni_x nobo(ru gyoku ichi|dan.

> The wind blows
> The azure's drifting clouds
> Clean away

> The moon rises
> To be the slate-blue mountains' gem,
> The perfect disc.

The meaning is: When the insubstantial clouds of delusion are dissolved, the moon that is Mind shines
out in the sky. When all is exhausted and cut off, the unique sun of light and life returns. "The azure"
is the sky.

612.　香爐峰雪揭簾見　遺愛寺鐘欹枕聞

Kō|ro|hō-no yuki-wa sudare-o_x kaka(gete mi,
I|ai|ji-no kane-wa makura-o_x sobadate(te ki(ku.　　[Bái Jū-yì]

Xiānglú Peak's snow
You lift the blind
To see

Yíai-sì's bell
You strain on your pillow
To hear.

A stanza about a mountain dwelling below Xiānglú [Incense Burner] Peak (north of Mount Lù). The state of mind of one of lofty character in a quiet retreat. And subtle images for THIS no-mind. [Yíai-sì: Bequeathed Love Temple; "pillow"—of wood.]

613.　鴛鴦繡出從君看　莫把金針度與人

En|nō-o nu(i ida(shite kimi-ga₂ mi(ru-ni₃ ma(kasu₁,
Kin|shin-o₃ to(tte₂ hito-ni₅ do|yo-suru-koto₄ naka(re₁.　　(Cliff 40Kn)

The pair of mandarin ducks
Embroidery is begun,
As you see

Don't take
The golden needle
To give to others.

Taking the golden needle to start embroidering your own beautiful work is fine, but the hidden technique of the golden needle must not be handed over to others. [A pair of mandarin ducks is an emblem of marital felicity.]

SIXTEEN

614.　仰之彌高鑽之彌堅　瞻之在前忽焉在後

Kore-o_x ao(geba iyoiyo taka(ku, kore-o_x ki(reba iyoiyo kata(shi,
Kore-o_x mi(te mae-ni_x a(ru-ka-to-sureba kotsu|en-to-shite shirie-ni_x a(ri.
(Analects 9X1)

The more you look up for it the higher it gets
The more you bore into it the more impenetrable it gets

Look for it in front of you
And suddenly it's behind you.

The Great Way, like an unbreakable kernel, is beyond conjecture or analysis, immmensely important, most precious. ["It": THIS matter—changing on the instant, in accord with circumstances.]

凡夫若知即是聖人　聖人若會即是凡夫

Bom|pu mo(shi shi(raba sunawa(chi ko(re sei|jin,
Sei|jin mo(shi e(seba sunawa(chi ko(re bom|pu.　(Mu 9C)

When an ordinary man *knows*
He's a sage

When a sage *gets it*
He's an ordinary man.

Clearly find the true Great Way, and such distinctions as ordinary man/holy man will turn out to be pointless. ["Knows": Attains realization; "gets it": Lives it in his "ordinary" life—is integrated with "It".]

616.

劍輪飛處日月沈輝　寶杖敵時乾坤失色

Ken|rin to(bu tokoro jitsu getsu hikari-o$_x$ shizu(me,
Hō jō teki-suru toki ken|kon iro-o$_x$ shis(su.　(Realm 6:6Vn)

Where the sword-whirl disc flies
It dims the sun and moon's brightness

When the jeweled staff strikes
It renders heaven and earth speechless.

The disc formed by the whirling sword and the staff encrusted with gems indicate that which is fundamental. Thus the fundamental Mind of enlightenment is revealed, and it's realized for good and all that sun and moon, heaven and earth, are reflections, images of light and shadow. ["Dims": Outshines; "renders speechless": Literally, "pales"—with fright.]

617.

天何言哉四時行焉　地何言哉百物生焉

Ten nani-o-ka i(wan [ya] shi|ji okona(waru [ ];
Chi nani-o-ka i(wan [ya] hyaku|motsu na(ru [ ].　(Analects 17XIX3; Cliff 47I)

Whatever Heaven may say
The four seasons pass—

Whatever Earth may say
All things come into being—

Even if Heaven doesn't speak, and Earth is silent too, the round of the four seasons goes on without fail, and all things are constantly coming into being. Natural, spontaneous, impeccable functioning.

618.

孤峰頂上嘯月眠雲　大洋海中翻波走浪

Ko|hō chō|jō tsuki-ni$_x$ usobu(ki kumo-ni$_x$ nemu(ru,
Tai|yō kai|chū nami-o$_x$ hirugae(shi nami-ni$_x$ hashi(ru.

Atop the solitary peak
He sings to the moon
And sleeps in the clouds

In the middle of the great ocean
He turns back the waves
And drives the billows before him.

The first part depicts the state of mind and heart of the true man, and the second his aspect of transforming and liberating samādhi on going out among people.

619.

白雲堆裏不見白雲　流水聲裏不聞流水

Haku|un tai|ri haku|un-o$_x$ mi[zu,
Ryū|sui sei|ri ryū|sui-o$_x$ ki(ka[zu.

In the midst of a white cloud-bank
You don't see the white cloud

Immersed in flowing water's sound
You don't hear the flowing water.

This speaks of the kind of samādhi, that of "no-mind," [in which no thoughts, no consciousness, interfere with the mind's action]. In the samādhi of life's suchness, of all united in one great body, there is neither seeing nor hearing. [See ZDNM, p. 126.]

620.

金以火試玉以石試　木以杖試人以言試

Kin-wa hi-o$_x$ mot(te kokoro(mi, tama-wa ishi-o$_x$ mot(te kokoro(mi,
Mizu-wa tsue-o$_x$ mot(te kokoro(mi, hito-wa gen-o$_x$ mot(te kokoro(mu.

Test gold with fire
Test gems with a stone
Test water with a pole
and
Test men with words.

For each thing there is something to test it with. Try saying *the* word, and a man's worth is realized at once.

621.

隔山見煙便知是火　隔墻見角便知是牛

Yama-o$_x$ heda(tete kemuri-o$_x$ mi(te sunawa(chi ko(re$_2$ hi-naru-koto-o$_3$ shi(ri$_1$,
Kaki-o$_x$ heda(tete tsuno-o$_x$ mi(te sunawa(chi ko(re$_2$ ushi-naru-koto-o$_3$ shi(ru$_1$.

(Cliff 1I)

Seeing smoke past the mountain
You know
There's fire

Seeing horns beyond the fence
You know
It must be an ox.

Bespeaks robed monks' tact, which springs from good sense and ability. The Great Matter of the fundamental is everywhere!

622.

高高峰頂立不露頂　深深海底行不濕脚

Kō kō-taru hō|chō-ni ta(tte itadaki-o$_x$ arawa(sa[zu,
Shin shin-taru kai|tei-ni yui(te ashi-o$_x$ uruo(sa[zu.　(Daie 9)

High, high the peak's summit
You stand on
Without exposing your head

Deep, deep the sea's bottom
You walk on
Without getting your feet wet.

Effective words on the fundamental. To neither stop at enlightenment nor defile yourself with worldly ties.

623.

十分爽氣兮清磨暑秋　一片閑雲兮遠分天水

Jū|bun-no sō|ki [ ] kiyo(ku sho|shū-o$_x$ ma-shi,
Ip|pen-no kan|un [ ] tō(ku ten|sui-o$_x$ waka(tsu.

Enough bracing air (!)
Clears autumn heat
Clean away

A thin drift of cloud (!)
Makes sky and sea
Markedly distinct.

A serene, cool and refreshing scene in early fall. And, still more, the present, ongoing, marvelous scene.

624.

蛇出一寸知其大與小　人出一言知其長與短

Hebi is|sun-o$_x$ izu(reba [sono]dai[to]shō-to-o$_x$ shi(ri,
Hito ichi|gen-o$_x$ ida(seba [sono]chō[to]tan-to-o$_x$ shi(ru.　　(Realm 4)

When a snake comes out
One inch,
Tell whether
It's big or small

When a man comes out with
Even a single word,
Tell whether
He's high-minded or petty.

When a snake sticks its head out a little, be able to tell its size; when a person speaks one word, to tell their worth. When one part is seen, to tell the value of the whole.

625.

雁過長空影沈寒水　雁無遺蹤意水無沈影心

Kari chō|kū-o$_x$ su(gite kage kan|sui-ni$_x$ shizu(mu,
Kari-ni i|shō-no$_2$ i$_3$ [naku]$_1$ mizu-ni chin|ei-no$_2$ shin$_3$ na(shi$_1$.

A wild goose
Passing the length of the sky
Casts a shadow
Into the cold water

The goose has no idea
Of leaving a trace,
The water no consciousness
Of the sinking through of the shadow.

The goose flies without conscious intention, the water reproduces its flight without conscious intention. Both effortlessly, unintentionally, leave no trace, retain no trace, of its whereabouts at all.

626.

德雲閑古錐　　幾下妙峰頂
儭他痴聖人　　擔雪共填井

Toku|un-no kan|ko|sui,
Iku(tabi-ka kuda(ru Myō|bu|chō,
Ta-no$_2$ chi|sei|jin-o$_3$ yato(tte$_1$,
Yuki-o$_x$ nina(tte tomo-ni sei-o$_x$ uzu(mu.   (Ranks 5)

Tokuun, the mild old gimlet!
   —Countless times he's gone all the way down from Wonder Peak's summit

Getting other idiot sages
  To help carry snow and fill up the well together.

Tokuun, concealing his own mind's vista, going down from the seat of enlightenment, carrying snow with the help of other foolish wise men, keeps at the hopeless task of filling up the well. Having come down among the commonalty, the foolish sage practices compassion ceaselessly. Tokuun meets Zenzai Dōji [Sudhana] in the "Chapter on Entering the Dharmadhātu" of the Wreath Sutra. [See #553.]

627.

樂民之樂者　　民亦樂其樂
憂民之憂者　　民亦憂其憂

Tami|[no]$_2$ tanoshi(mi-o$_3$ tanoshi(mu$_1$ mono-wa
Tami-mo mata [sono]$_2$ tanoshi(mi-o$_3$ tanoshi(mu$_1$,
Tami|[no]$_2$ uree-o$_3$ ure(uru$_1$ mono-wa
Tami-mo mata [sono]$_2$ uree-o$_3$ ure(u$_1$.

One who delights in [his] people's joy [is one whose]
  People also delight in his joy

One who grieves over [his] people's suffering [is one whose]
  People also grieve over his suffering.

The sovereign and his people at one, concord between the high and the low. Peace, harmony and calm as the foundation of a nation, of a community . . .

628.

若人欲了知　　三世一切佛
應觀法界性　　一切唯心造

Mo(shi hito san|ze$_3$ is|sai-no$_4$ hotoke-o$_5$ ryō|chi(sen-to$_2$ hos(shinaba$_1$,
Masa-ni hok|kai|shō-wa$_2$ is|sai$_3$ yui|shin$_4$ zō-nari-to$_5$ kan-subeshi$_1$.   (Wreath 19V)

If you want to thoroughly know
  All Buddhas, past, present and future

Be clear about this world's real nature
  —That [one's own] Mind alone creates the totality and every thing.

When you clearly see this world's real nature: That everything is produced by the One Mind—then you must accept the fact that even what we call all the Buddhas, in their past, present and future aspects, are produced by this One Mind! This world's real nature may be: (1) imprisonment—in the earth: Hell or purgatory, (2) being a preta (hungry ghost), (3) born an animal, (4) an asura (warring titanic enemy of the gods), (5) a human, (6) a god, (7) a śrāvaka (hearer of the Dharma), (8) a Pratyeka-Buddha (seeker by and for himself), (9) a Bodhisattva, and (10) a Buddha. ["Every thing"—deeds, events, facts . . .]

菩提元無樹　明鏡亦非臺
本來無一物　何處惹塵埃

Bo|dai moto ju$_x$ na(shi,
Mei|kyō mata tai-ni$_x$ [arazu],
Hon|rai mu|ichi|motsu,
Izure-no tokoro-ni-ka jin|ai-o$_x$ hi(kan.　　(Platform 8)

Bodhi never had a tree
Nor that bright mirror any stand.

Fundamentally not a thing exists;
Where could dust adhere?

This is the verse of the Sixth Patriarch, Enō Daishi [Great-master], when he was still able to stay and be under the Fifth Patriarch, in which he succeeded in presenting his own insight in responding to the verse of the Head Monk, Shén-xiù. This single verse manifests Enō Daishi's Zen. [See phrases #193 and #196.]

630.

趙州露刃劍　寒霜光焰焰
僅擬問如何　分身作兩段

Jō|shū-no ro|jin|ken,
Kan|sō hikari en en,
Wazu(ka-ni i|kan-to$_3$ to(wan-to$_2$ gi-sureba$_1$,
Mi-o$_x$ waka(tte ryō|dan-to$_x$ na(ru.

Jōshū's sword of impermanence,
Coldly glittering, fiery, blazing

Slightly waver into considering questions of how and why
And your body is cut in two!

This phrase of Goso Hōen Zenji is in praise of the words of Jōshū in Case 1 of *Mumonkan*, saying that a dog has *Mu* [literally, "no"] Buddha-nature. It is a compassionate suggestion—that the single word "*mu*" may be spoken of figuratively as the sword of impermanence.

TWENTY-TWO

631.

有時拈一莖草作丈六金身
有時拈丈六金身作一莖草

A(ru toki-wa ik|kyō|sō-o$_x$ nen(jite jō|roku-no$_2$ kon|jin-to$_3$ na(shi$_1$,
A(ru toki-wa jō|roku-no$_2$ kon|jin-o$_3$ nen(jite$_1$ ik|kyō|sō-to$_x$ na(su.　　(Cliff 8I)

At times, a blade of grass
Is the sixteen-foot Golden Body

Other times, the sixteen-foot Golden Body
Is a blade of grass.

With your state of mind on the rise, you'll have such partial freedom—and also the subtle sense that even birth-and-death, delusion-and-distress, are exactly nirvāṇa.

BIBLIOGRAPHY

*Acronyms (***ZD, PD,** ... *) refer to the* Modern and Reference Works *section. After each source citation is a reference to a description of the source [the numbers refer to pages]. Translations from the source are then given in reverse chronological order: latest first. The table following the translations is an index from the source to the phrases in this book: The numbers following the "/" refer to the phrases; if there is a blank space before the "/" then either the source is not divided into sections or the editor has not found these phrases in the source.*

PRINCIPAL SOURCES:

Cliff 碧巖錄 Hekigan Roku *The Blue Cliff Record* **ZD** 356-8

Koans 11, 51 and 73 are in **PD**.

Koans 1, 2, 4-6, 27 and 73 are in **GW**.

Complete translation: Thomas and J.C. Cleary, *The Blue Cliff Record* (Boston: Shambala, 1977).

The entire work, but with the translator's own notes in place of the original notes and commentaries, is in **TZC**.

Case 1 (without notes or commentaries) and Case 2, translated by D.T. Suzuki, are in **TZBM**, p. 101-103, and **EBN** I,2, September, 1966, p. 12-20, respectively.

All 100 koans, but with the translator's "interpretations" in place of notes or commentary: R.D.M. Shaw, D.D., *The Blue Cliff Records:* The Hekigan Roku (London: Michael Joseph, 1961).

Incomplete German translation: Wilhelm Gundert, *Bi-yän-lu:* Meister Yüan-wu's Niederschrift von der Smaragdenen Felswand: Band I, Koans 1-30 [1-33]; Band 2, Koans 31-50 [34-50] (München: Carl Hanser, 1960, 1967 [2. Auflage 1977, 1981]).

Case 88, translated by D.T. Suzuki, is in **MZB**, p. 120-127.

Case 55, translated by D.T. Suzuki, is in **EZB2**, p. 256-264.

Most of the 100 Cases begin with an Introduction (I). Then comes the Koan (K), the case proper, with interlinear notes (Kn) and commentary (Kc) and then a Verse (V) [or Verses (V1, V2)] with interlinear notes (Vn) and commentary (Vc).

1I/119 123 145 621	5I/142	8Kc/61	16I/597	25K/574
K/30 114	K/134	V/100 109 230	K/105	V/340 542
Kc/126 174	Kn/179	9Kc/379	Kc/171	26K/202
V/30 322	V/247 333	V/325	17K/108 206	Kc/367
Vc/434	6K/192	10Kn/117	18K/29 242	V/359
2I/135	Kn/216 225 347	11Kn/96	Kn/116	27K/176
K/405	V/252 278 563	12V/256	Kc/132	Vn/416
Kc/96	Vn/218	13I/292	19Vn/66	28V/215
Vn/86 111	Vc/396	K/213	20I/388	30K/258
3K/235	7I/101 404	14Kc/95 161 167	V2/351 548	31I/379
V/235 326	Kc/105 195	V/36	V2n/41 194	32V/559
4K/37 99 154	V/532 579	15Kc/170	23K/54	33V/298
Kn/56 401	8I/49 379 631	V/291 305	24I/172 402	
V/37	K/23		Kn/293	
Vn/127	Kn/71			

34K/69	42K/380	55K/31	76Kn/83	90I/404 Kn/211
35K/97 224 369 546	43K/499 Kc/554 Vc/104	57K/377	78Vn/358	93V/286
36K/284 441 V/441 Vn/159	44K/70	58K/96	79K/492 Kn/165	96V1/207 V1c/477
37K/365 V/365 521 Vn/175	45V/552	60Kn/110 Vn/387	80K/233	98K/20 V/20 Vc/130
38K/13 Kn/93 Kc/603	47I/617 Kn/61 V/515	61Kc/529	82K/445	99Kc/584
40I/169 K/18 Kn/613 Vn/564	49V/267	62I/16 V/16 47 308	83K/227 370 Kn/225 276	100K/329 V/36 329
	50K/257	66K/10 Vn/239	84Kc/133	
	51K/9 58 514 V/60 544	70V/541	86K/184 Kn/82	
	53Kn/503 V/345	73K/253 V/63 253 309	87K/474	
		75K/128	89K/210	

Mu 無門關 Mumonkan *The Gateless Barrier*   Original in **Z**; **ZD** 342-4

Koans 1, 17, 44-46 and 48 are in **PD**.

Koans 1-4, 9, 17-19, 21, 24, 29, 30 and 39 are in **GW**.

The entire work, with extensive footnotes by the translator, is in **TZC**.

A complete translation, each section followed by a "comment," actually a complete *teisho* [Zen discourse], is *Zen Comments on the Mumonkan* by Shibayama Zenkei Roshi, translated by Sumiko Kudo (New York: Harper & Row, 1974; Mentor, 1975).

The text in the original Chinese, each section followed by R.H. Blyth's translation and extensive commentary, is **ZZC4**.

A free translation of the entire text is that of Nyogen Senzaki and Paul Reps, *The Gateless Gate* (first published in 1934), in **ZFZB**.

48 Koans (K), each with a Commentary (C) and a Verse (V); the Preface also contains a Verse.

Preface/166 V/376	10K/580	20C/343 V/334	36K/482 V/482
1K/14 397 V/92	11V/243	22C/576	37K/188 C/368
2K/87 89	12K/6 55 C/17 V/584	23K/121 219	41C/5 348
3V/559	13K/34	24K/560	43V/91
4C/371	15K/12 79 V/328	30K/103	44C/452
6K/115 389 393 C/234	18V/426	31K/80	46K/332 591 V/179
9C/434 615	19K/187 C/96 144	33K/173	47K/118
		35V/414	

Rinzai 臨濟錄 Rinzai Roku *The Record of Rinzai* **ZD** 346-7

Section 2XII is translated in **GW**.

The Zen Teachings of Master Lin-chi (Boston & London: Shambala, 1993), translated by Burton Watson, is complete, and includes two somewhat suspect sections as an appendix—and a glossary.

The Zen Teaching of Rinzai (Berkeley: Shambala, 1976), translated by Irmgard Schloegl, is complete except for the original Preface.

The Record of Lin-chi (Kyoto: The Institute for Zen Studies, 1975), translated by Ruth F. Sasaki [and other scholars, Japanese and American], is a complete translation including the original Chinese text as established by the translators.

Sections from the Discourses are in **ZBP**, p. 33-43.

Most of Section 1X, translated by D.T. Suzuki, is in **EZB3** (first published in 1953).

Part of Section 1X, translated by D.T. Suzuki and first published in the Chicago Review in 1948, is in **AZ**.

A translation of Section 3I, made by D.T. Suzuki in 1939, is in **EZB2**.

The Sasaki translation is in three parts: Discourses (1), Critical Examinations (2) and Record of Pilgrimages (3) followed by the Preface. The letters after Section 1XVIII denote subsections, the number of paragraphs in each being: a:11, b:4, c:5, d:5 (+ 6 lines), e:(3 lines +) 6, f:5, g:3, h:7, i:4.

Preface/8 21 78 137	1XIII/43 158	2I/8 53 78	3I/8 222
178 222 385 391	XIV/27 130	II/8	II/525
	XVI/138 413	IV/8	VI/52 84
1I/8 90	XVII/65 138	V/19	IX/53
II/28 51	XVIIIa/33 43 138	VII/19 43	XII/49 51
III/47 137 178	c/33 50 175 410	IX/8	XIII/8 35 555
IV/8 93 112	d/33 43 450 489	X/8	XIX/339 381 603
V/8	f/138	XII/411	XXI/8
VI/90 98 148	h/43 475	XIII/4	
VII/46	i/65	XIV/8	
VIII/547	XIX/27	XVI/28	
IX/531	XX/27 43 107	XX/8 117 212 255	
X/43 116 321	XXII/43 46 81 362	XXI/8	
408 587		XXIII/8	
XI/201			
XII/113 157 168			
413			

OTHER SOURCES:

Analects 論語 Rongo *The Analects [of Confucius]*
   In: Ezra Pound, *Confucius* (New York: New Directions, 1951)
   Arthur Waley, *The Analects of Confucius* (1938)
   In: James Legge, *Confucius* (1893; republished in New York: Dover, 1971)
   20 Books with Chapters [of one or more numbered verses] in Roman Numerals.
  4VIII/312 4XV/228 4XXV/302 7XXI/274 7XXIII/181 9X1/614 17XIX3/617

Arsenal 大慧武庫 Daie Buko *Dà-huì's Arsenal* **ZD** 410-11
/46 231 251

Changes 易經 Ekikyō *The Book of Changes* **ZD** 364-5
Richard Wilhelm, The I Ching or Book of Changes, translated by Cary F. Baynes
(Princeton University Press, 1967)
/417

Chūhō 中峰廣錄 Chūhō Kōroku *The Comprehensive Record of Chūhō* **ZD** 411
/266 297 361

Compendium 五燈會元 Gotō Egen *Compendium of the Five Lamps*
[of **Lamp** *and four similar works]* **ZD** 429-30
In 20 Sections.
5/585 601 7/378 8/524 20/517 608 18/526 604 /214 383 466 491

Comprehensive 普燈錄 Futō Roku *Comprehensive Record of the*
[Transmission of the] Lamp **ZD** 348-9
In 33 Sections.
2/565 5/493 11/456 13/249 14/2 16/300 609 21/549 27/431 28/265 29/248 349 551
/245 454

Dào 老子、道德經 Rōshi, Dōtoku Kyō *Lǎo Zi, Dào Dé Jing*
Witter Bynner, *The Way of Life According to Lao Tzu*
(New York: Capricorn Books, 1962)
Arthur Waley, *The Way and Its Power* (New York: Grove Press, 1958)
In 81 Chapters.
4,56/149

Daie 大慧語錄 Daie Goroku *The Record of Dà-huì* **ZD** 409-10
In 30 Sections.
9/622 /2 357 519 601 610

Dhammapada *The Way of the Dharma* Pali verses spoken by the Buddha
P. Lal, *The Dhammapada* (New York: Farrar, Straus & Giroux, 1967)
Narada Thera, *The Dhammapada* (London: John Murray, 1954; distributed
by Paragon Book Gallery, New York)
In XXVI Chapters: 423 Verses—as in Narada Thera's translation.
XV:204/48

Diamond 金剛經 Kongo Kyō *The Diamond Sutra* **ZD** 420-1
Zenrin R. Lewis, *The Diamond Sutra* (Jacksonville, FL: Zen Sangha Press, 1995)
Eido Shimano Roshi and students, *The Diamond Sutra,* Dialogue Version
(New York: The Zen Studies Society, 1990)
In: **BWB** [This translation is from the Sanskrit, the others from the Chinese]
In: **DSSHN**
In: **MZB**—translation of the first half and of extracts from the second half
by D.T. Suzuki, p. 38-50
In 32 Chapters.
1/39 10/384 14,23/44

Equanimity 從容錄 Shōyō Roku *The Record of [the Hermitage of]*
Equanimity **ZD** 425-6
Thomas Cleary, *Book of Serenity* (Hudson, NY: Lindisfarne Press, 1990)
Consists of koans in the form and style of **Cliff***, so the same notation is used here.*
2K/30 114 V/114 3K/494 8K,Kc/87 89 10K/80 11K,Kc/33 12Vn/172 23Vn/176
31K227 370 Kn/301 35K,Kc/414 36K,V/235 38K/47 137 178 41K/122 Kn/109 44Kn/93
47K/188 48K/26 50K/58 52Kn/381 602 V/221 56Vn/172 59Kn/416
64K,Vn/17 341 Kn/84 V/17 65K,Kn,V/306 67Vn/184 69K/529 71K/23 75Kn/93 80K/206
83Kn/249 85Vn/176 86Kn/93 87Vn,91Vn/480 98Kn/224 99K,V/257 /344

Eye 人天眼目 Ninden Gammoku *The Eye of Men and Gods* **WI** 58; **ZD** 365
In 6 Sections.
1/295 314 327 447 469 2/277 307 3/331 /22 435 459

Faith 信心銘 *Shinjin Mei* On Faith in Mind Original in: ZZ
In: **ENS**
In: **MZB**, p. 76-82, translated by D.T. Suzuki; reprinted in **DS**, p. 31-6
*In 31 Stanzas: 146 (4-character) Lines [as in **MZB**]*
11:1,2/407 21:4/158 407 31:3/163

Five Houses 五家正宗賛 Goke Shōjū San *Praise for the Five Sects of the
True School* **WI** 37; **ZD** 426-7
/57 59 64

Hán-shān 寒山詩 Kanzan Shi *The Poems of Hán-shān ("Cold Mountain")*
David Hawkes discusses Hán-shān and the ancient introduction to the poems, with
tables to compare the original and the translations, in his review of the Watson
translation: *Journal of the American Oriental Society*, 82.4 (1962),p.596-9.
Burton Watson, *Cold Mountain:* 100 Poems by the T'ang Poet Han-shan
(New York: Grove Press, 1962)
In: Gary Snyder, *Riprap, and Cold Mountain Poems* (San Francisco: Four Seasons
Foundation, 1965)—24 poems; reprinted in Cyril Birch, ed., *Anthology of Chinese
Literature* (New York: Grove Press, 1965), p. 194-202.
*Introduction [=preface] and 313 Poems (here the numbers are those of the Snyder
translation).*
I/507 1/467 5/430 449 /203 436

Heart 般若心經 Hannya Shingyō *The Heart [of Wisdom] Sutra* **ZD** 381-3
In: **SB**, p. 3-4 (English) and p. 5 (Sino-Japanese)
In: **Poison**
In: **BWB**
/18 406

Huáng-bò 傳心法要 [Ōbaku] Denshin Hōyō *Huáng-bò's Essentials of the
Dharma: On the Transmission of Mind*
A selection from the following translation is in **SB**, p. 38-40.
John Blofeld, *The Zen Teaching of Huang Po:* On the Transmission of Mind
(New York: Grove Press, 1958)
In two "Records": I: 36 Sections; II: 56 Sections.
I:32/32 I:35/32 II:26/32 46

Hymn 正信念佛偈 Shōshin Nembutsu Ge *Hymn on the Nembutsu of the
Right Faith*
In: D.T. Suzuki, The Kyōgyōshinshō: *The Collection of Passages Expounding the True
Teaching, Living, Faith and Realizing of the Pure Land* —by Shinran Shonin,
p. 75-81.
In 19 Sections [as in the above translation].
6/280

Jowa 貞和集 Jōwa Shū *The Jowa [Japanese era: 1345-9] Collection*
ZGD 593d
In 10 Sections.
1/77 590 3/531 7/486 8/268 275 9/263 269 589 10/350

Kidō 虛堂録 Kidō Roku *The Record of Xūtáng* **ZD** 361-2
See Norman Waddell, "Talks by Hakuin Introductory to Lectures on the Records of
Old Sokko [=**Kidō**] (*Sokkō-Roku Kaien Fusetsu*)" in **EBN** XVIII2, 79-92; XIX2, 75-
84; XX2, 89-99; XXI1, 101-117; XXII2, 85-104; XXIII, [?]; and XXIV1, 97-122
Yoel Hoffman, *Every End Exposed:* The 100 Perfect Koans of Master Kido
(Brookline, MA: Autumn Press, 1977; distr. by Random House) is a translation of
the first half of Section 6.
In 10 Sections.
1/75 310 476 494 495 511 2/125 185 246 313 4/250 5/513 7/592 8/464 481
/156 453 495

Lamp 景徳傳燈録 Keitoku Dentō Roku *The Keitoku [Chinese era] Record*
of the Transmission of the Lamp **ZD** 350-2
The first 10 sections: Ogata Sohaku, *The Transmission of the Lamp (Ching Te*
Ch'uanTeng Lu) [Typescript copy bound in 2 vols., 1971]
19 entries are in Chang Chung-yuan, *Original Teachings of Ch'an Buddhism*
(New York: Pantheon div. of Random House, 1969).
Selected entries are in **CZT2**.
In 30 Sections, each consisting of entries (records of individual masters).
2/450 489 5/33 11/545 15/585 16/154 17/303 20/104 23/470 25/382

Lotus 妙法蓮華經 Myōhō Renge Kyō *The Sutra of the Lotus*
of the Wonderful Law **ZD** 388-90
In: *The Threefold Lotus Sutra,* tr. by Kato Bunno et al. (New York & Tokyo:
Weatherhill/Kosei, 1975)
28 Chapters, each consisting of prose and then Verse sections.
2/177 25V/189

Mirror 寶鏡三昧 Hōkyō Zammai *The Jeweled-Mirror Samadhi*
ZD 379-81; the original is in **ZZ**.
In: **TS**, p. 39-42; **ZZC2**, p. 152-8; and **CZT2**, p. 149-154
In 94 (4-character) Lines.
5/213 412 6/412 91,92/395

Nirvāṇa 涅槃經 Nehan Gyō *The [Mahāpari]nirvāṇa sūtra* **SH** 329a
/88 501

Ox 十牛図 Jūgyū Zu *The Ten Oxherding Pictures* **ZD** 322; the original is in **ZZ**.
In: **ZFZB**, p. 130-155
In: **MZB**, p. 127-134
Each picture has a Commentary and Verse by Kakuan and additional Verses V2
and V3 by others; neither V2 nor V3 are included in the above translations.
9V/320 9V2/566

Platform 六祖壇經 Rokuso Dangyō *The Sixth Patriarch's Platform Sutra*
ZD 402-4
Philip B. Yampolsky, *The Platform Sutra of the Sixth Patriarch* (New York:
Columbia Univ. Press, 1967)
Wing-tsit Chan, *The Platform Scripture* (New York: St. John's Univ. Press, 1963)
Excerpts in: **MZB**, p. 82-9
Translated by A.F. Price in: **DSSHN**
In 57 Chapters.
6/193 8/196 629 11/219 14/85   /346

Poison 毒語心經 Dokugo Shingyō *[Hakuin Zenji's] Poison Words on the
Heart Sutra* Original is in **ZZ**.
    Norman Waddell, "Zen Master Hakuin's Poison Words for the Heart,"
      EB XIII2, p. 73-114
    41 Phrases: 1 introductory, the rest comprising **Heart**, *each with Hakuin's Commentary
and Verse.*
2C/373 4C/216 5C/58 485 584 8C/547 9V/53 13C/172 22C/594 23C/471

Ranks 五位頌 Goi-no Jū *Verses on the Five Ranks,* by Tōzan Ryōkai
      ZBP 59-76; **ZD** 309; original, with commentary by Hakuin, is in **Z.**
    In: **ZD**, p. 63-72 [with the commentary by Hakuin]
    5 Verses.
4/285 299 5/190 626

Realm 槐安國語 Kaiankoku Go *Tales from the Realm of Locust-tree
Tranquility,* by Hakuin Ekaku **ZD** 366-7
    In 7: Sections. Sections 5:, 6: and 7: consist of koans in the form and style of **Cliff**, *so
the same notation is used here.*
1:/136 363 419 425 428 523 568 573 599
2:/3 424 485 585
3:/353
4:/198 200 311 380 445 457 522 581 588 593 606 624
5:6V/553 7K/213 11Kn/605 11Vn/560 14/66 15/365 19/227 370 23Vn/596
    5:/316 330 409 488 518 520 602
6:1Vc/229 3Kn/223 5V/443 6Vn/616
    6:/490 516
7:/147

Song 證道歌 Shōdōka *Song of Enlightenment* **DCZ** 5, 82; the original is in **ZZ**.
    In: **MZB**, p. 89-103
    In 56 Stanzas: —each of 4-12 Lines [as in **MZB**].
1:1/21 45 336 20:1/254 23:8/271 24:5/244 56:1,2/498

Spur 禪關策進 Zenkan Sakushin *Whips to Spur [the Student on] Through
the Zen Barrier* **WI** I43; **ZD** 341-2
    Quoted: **TZBM**, p. xix; **WI** I44; **ZD**, p. 316
/106

Táng 唐詩 Táng-dynasty poems
    A selection of original poems is in: Wu-chi Liu and Irving Yucheng Lo, eds.,
      K'uei Yeh Chi (Bloomington, IN: Indiana University Press, 1976).
    Translation of *K'uei Yeh Chi:* Liu and Lo, eds., *Sunflower Splendor:* Three
      Thousand Years of Chinese Poetry (Bloomington: Indiana University Press, 1975)
    A translation of the "standard" anthology with the original below each translated
      poem: Innes Herdan, *300 T'ang Poems*
    (New York & Taiwan: The Far East Book Co., 1973)
    A selection of such poems, translated by Peter A. Boodberg, is in **CBWAP**.
    The reference marked "C:" is to a Cedule number of **CBWAP**; *those marked "T:" are to
Page numbers in Herdan,* 300 T'ang Poems.
C:12,T:379/472 T:257/480 T:286/484 T:386/439 455 T:426/570
    /337 433 444 446 538 540 560 561 582 594 612

Ummon 雲門廣錄 Ummon Kōroku *The Comprehensive Record of Ummon*
　　UA 239-41; **ZD** 432-3
　　UA is an extensive partial translation.
　　[In 3 Sections:] 285 Selected subsections, the latter as in **UA**.
7/46 81 20/198 22/157 26/257 44/13 46/46 143 312 48/25 74/46 78/53 79/47 81/6 83/206
　　84/46 94/8 95/176
114/215 120/603 127/175 138,141/46 145/8 148/103 150/13 151/53 152/35 43 153/35
　　154/35 58 156/53 157/35 160/6 161/8 50 53 162,163/35 164/35 492 169/35 170/53
　　171/50 492 172,174/33 176/38 178/33 181/8 184/53 185/50 51 186/23 187/33 188/13
　　189/53 192/53 193,196/33 198/33 53 199/53 301
203/50 205/33 207/492 208/33 210/43 213/53 214/9 33 217/50 218/377 219,220/33 221/50
　　223/53 227 370 224-226/33 228-229/53 231/47 232/53 233,234/53 235/33 358 236/33
　　237/47 239/53 241/12 242/53 243/192 245/53 184 246/53 248-250/53 251/33 252,254/53
　　255/33 50 256/33 257,258/53 264/33 266/33 265/13 53 267/184 268-271/33 272/53
　　273/33 50 79 274/13 275/13 33 277/33 278/53 279/13 33 50 280/33 50 53 281/13 53
　　282/33 53 283/33 50 53 284/33 285/50
　　　1:/162　2:/375　　/290 350 470

Vimalakirti 維摩經 Yuima Kyō *The Vima[lakirti-nirdeśa] Sūtra* **ZD** 421-4
　HTV
　　Charles Luk, *The Vimalakirti Nirdesa Sutra* (Berkeley: Shambala, 1972)
　　In 14 Chapters.
9/26 /204

Wreath 華嚴經 Kegon Kyō *The Avatamsaka Sutra, The Wreath Sutra, The Great Comprehensive Sutra on the Adornments of Buddha* The Chinese
　　original: **T**, # 279: vol. 10, p. 1-441; **ZD** 337-41
　　Bhikshuni Heng Hsien, *The Flower Adornment Sutra*—being published in 75-100
　　volumes with commentaries by Master Hsuan Hua (San Francisco: The Buddhist
　　Text Translation Society).
　　Cleary, Thomas F., *The Flower Ornament Scripture*
　　(Boulder: Shambala, 1984 [I], 1986 [II]).
　　Excerpts in: Cook, Francis H., *Hua-yen Buddhism* (University Park:
　　Pennsylvania State University Press, 1977).
　　In 39 Chapters, most containing parts in Verse.
19V/628 /142

Zen 禪林類聚 Zenrin Ruishū *The Collection, Grouped in Classes,*
　of the Zen Grove **ZGD** 710a
　　All the "interviews," "dialogues" and "stories" in **TZBM** are taken from this work.
　　In 20 Sections.
2/180 191 221 487 5/131 183 6/209 319 7/423 8/354 411 577 9/222 11/512 12/1 470
　　16/94 223　/355

REFERENCE AND MODERN WORKS

AZ *The Awakening of Zen*, by D.T. Suzuki (Boulder: Prajna Press, 1980).
BGD 佛教語大辭典 Bukkyogo Daijiten *Great Dictionary of Buddhist Terms.* 3 vols.,
　　edited by Nakamura Hajime (Tokyo Shoseki, 1975).
BWB *Buddhist Wisdom Books*, containing The Diamond Sutra and the Heart Sutra,
　　translated [from the Sanskrit] and explained by Edward Conze
　　(New York: Harper & Row, 1972).
CBWAP *Cedules From a Berkeley Workshop in Asiatic Philology*, published by Peter A.
　　Boodberg in 1954-5. 54 numbered sheets. Numbers 1-14 and 16-34 are reprinted
　　in **SWPAB**.

116

CY *Cat's Yawn:* The 13 Numbers from 1940 and 1941, by Sasaki Shigetsu (Sokei-an) (New York: The First Zen Institute of America, 1947).
  *Most Numbers include a "Zenrin Collection" section: phrases translated by Sokei-an from **ZRKS**-type books, often with the original context given.*
I,1/445 I,2/198 453 479 I,3/198 I,10/484 I,12/441 600   II,1/520

CZT1,2,3 *Ch'an and Zen Teaching* (Series 1,2,3), translated and edited by Charles Luk (London: Rider & Co., 1960, 1961, 1962).

DCZ *The Development of Chinese Zen After the Sixth Patriarch*, by H. Dumoulin, S.J.; translated by Ruth F. Sasaki (New York: First Zen Institute of America, 1953).

DS *Daily Sutras For Chanting and Recitation.* (New York: The Zen Studies Society, 1982).

DSSHN *The Diamond Sutra and the Sutra of Hui Neng*, tr. by A.F. Price and Wong Mou-lam respectively (Boston: Shambala, 1967, 1990).

EB[N] *The Eastern Buddhist [New Series].* A biannual journal for the study of Mahayana Buddhism founded by D.T. Suzuki and published in Kyoto.

ENS *The Eye Never Sleeps:* Striking to the Heart of Zen, by Dennis Genpo Merzel (Boston: Shambala, 1991)

EZB1,2,3 *Essays in Zen Buddhism*, 1st, 2nd and 3rd Series, by D.T. Suzuki (New York: Grove Press, 1961 [1]; Weiser, 1971 [2 & 3]).

GW *Golden Wind:* Zen Talks, by Eido Shimano Roshi (Tokyo: Japan Publications, 1979, 1992).

H *Handbook of Japanese Grammar*, Revised Edition, by Harold G. Henderson (New York: Houghton Mifflin, 1948).

HTV *The Holy Teaching of Vimalakirti:* A Mahayana Scripture, translated by Robert A.F. Thurman (University Park, PA, & London: The PA State Univ. Press, 1976).
  Includes a 3-part glossary: (1) Sanskrit Terms, (2) Numerical Categories, and (3) Technical Terms including extensive discussions of all difficult terms.

KD *Analytic Dictionary of Chinese and Sino-Japanese*, by Bernhard Karlgren (New York: Dover, 1974).

M *Mathew's Chinese-English Dictionary*, Revised American Edition, by R.H. Mathews (Cambridge, MA: Harvard Univ. Press, 1943).

MZB *Manual of Zen Buddhism*, by D.T. Suzuki (New York: Grove Press, 1960).

N *Japanese-English Character Dictionary*, 2nd Revised Edition, by Andrew N. Nelson (Rutland, VT, & Tokyo: Tuttle, 1974).

PD *Points of Departure:* Zen Buddhism with a Rinzai View, by Eido T. Shimano [Roshi] (Livingston Manor, NY: The Zen Studies Society Press, 1991)

RJ *Reading Japanese*, by E.H. Jorden and H.I. Chaplin (New Haven and London: Yale Univ. Press, 1976).

SH *A Dictionary of Chinese Buddhist Terms* —with Sanskrit Equivalents and a Sanskrit-Pali Index, by W.E. Soothill and L. Hodous (Taipei: Ch'eng-wen, 1969).

SWPAB *Selected Works of P.A. Boodberg,* compiled by Alvin P. Cohen
(Berkeley: University of California Press, 1979).

T 大正新修大藏經 Taishō Shinshū Daizōkyō, *The Taishō-Era New Compilation
of the Tripitaka,* in 100 vols. (Tokyo: Taishō Issaikyō Kankōkai, 1924-34).

TS *Timeless Spring:* A Soto Zen Anthology, edited and translated by Thomas Cleary
(New York, Weatherhill, 1980).

TZBM *The Training of the Zen Buddhist Monk,* by D.T. Suzuki
(New York: University Books, 1965).

TZC *Two Zen Classics:* Mumonkan and Hekiganroku, translated with commentaries
by Katsuki Sekida; edited and introduced by A.V. Grimstone
(New York: Weatherhill, 1977).

UA *Master Yunmen:* From the Record of the Chan Master "Gate of the Clouds,"
translated, edited, and with an introduction by Urs App
(New York: Kodansha International, 1994).

WI "Wild Ivy: The Spiritual Autobiography of Hakuin Ekaku," (I): **EBN** XV2,
p. 71-109; (II) **EBN** XVI1, p. 107-139—translated by Norman Waddell.
References to this work are footnote numbers.

Z[Z] 塗毒鼓〔續篇〕 Zudokko [Zokuhen], *The Poison-painted Drum [Supplementary
Volume]* (Kyoto: Kennin Sodo, 1917 [1922]) **ZD** 434.

ZBP *Zen Buddhism and Psychoanalysis,* by D.T. Suzuki, Erich Fromm and Richard
DeMartino (New York: Grove Press, 1963; Harper and Row, 1970).

ZD *Zen Dust:* The History of the Koan and Koan Study in Rinzai Zen,
by Isshu Miura and Ruth Fuller Sasaki (New York: Harcourt Brace, 1966).
Parts I: History, II: Koan Study, and III: Selections from **ZRKS** *and Drawings by Hakuin,
were published as* The Zen Koan *(Harcourt Brace, 1965). Extensive notes, bibliography,
and indexes. All references to this work are page numbers.*

ZDNM *The Zen Doctrine of No Mind,* by D.T. Suzuki (New York: Weiser, 1972).

ZF *A Zen Forest:* Sayings of the Masters, tr. by Soiku Shigematsu
(New York: Weatherhill, 1981).
"Characters and Romanization" appendix; "Bibliographical Note" of Zen sayings books.

ZFZB *Zen Flesh, Zen Bones,* compiled by Paul Reps
(Rutland and Tokyo: Tuttle, 1957; Garden City, NY: Doubleday, n.d.).
In 3 Sections—I: 101 Zen Stories; II: The Gateless Gate [a translation of **Mu***];
and III: Centering.*
I83/364

ZGD 禪學大辭典 Zengaku Daijiten *Great Zen Studies Dictionary* (3 vols.),
edited by Zengaku Daijiten Hensanjo (Tokyo: Taishukan Shoten, 1978).

ZRKS 禪林句集 Zenrin Kushū, *Zen Grove Phrase Collection* (Revised Edition),
selected and translated into Japanese with an introduction and commentaries by
Shibayama Zenkei (Kyoto: Kichūdō, 1978).

ZZC *Zen and Zen Classics,* Vols. 1-5, by R.H. Blyth
(Tokyo: Hokuseido, 1960, 1964, 1970, 1966, 1964).

JAPANESE INDEX

This index begins on page 130. The numbers below are phrase numbers.

梅邊殘月無疎影竹裏清風有落花 573

ハク
白雲盡處是青山行人更在青山外 590

ヒ

ビ
毘婆尸佛早留心直到如今不得妙 576

ヒャク
百尺竿頭進一歩十方刹土現全身 591

フ

フ
不見西湖林處士一生受用只梅花 533

フウ
風吹不動天邊月雪壓難摧磵底松 609

フウ
風吹碧落浮雲盡月上青山玉一團 611

フウ
風吹柳絮毛毬走雨打梨花蛺蝶飛 610

ミ

ミョウ
妙峰孤頂難人到只看白雲飛又歸 553

ム

ム
無一物中無盡藏有花有月有樓臺 583

ム
無始劫來生死本痴人喚作本來人 584

ラ

ラク
落花有意隨流水流水無情送落花 602

リ

リョウ
良藥苦口利於病忠言逆耳利於行 598

リョウ
兩岸猿聲啼不住輕舟已過萬重山 538

ロ

ロ
路逢劍客須呈劍不是詩人莫獻詩 603

十 六 字 （八言對）

カ

カク
隔山見煙便知是火隔墻見角便知是牛 621

キ

ギョウ
仰之彌高鑽之彌堅瞻之在前忽焉在後 614

ザ 坐斷毘盧頂顙曽不見有佛祖 497

シ
ショ 處處眞處處眞塵塵盡本來人 509

ス
スイ 雖與我同條生不與我同條死 514

セ
セン 戰戰兢兢如臨深淵如履薄氷 500

ツ
ソウ 爭如著衣喫飯此外更無佛祖 505

タ
タイ 大象不遊兔徑大悟不拘小節 498

チ
チク 逐鹿者不見山攫金者不見人 511
タツ 達磨不來東土二祖不往西天 512
タツ 達磨不居少室六祖不住曹溪 513

ニ
チョウ 聽鐘知有古寺見烟覺有野村 508
ニュウ 入息不居陰界出息不涉萬緣 494

フ
フ 父母所生鼻孔却在別人手裏 503
フ 父有迷子之訣子有打爺之拳 502

ヨ
ブン 文殊不識寒山普賢不識拾得 507
ヨク 欲識佛性義理當觀時節因緣 501

十四字 （七言對）

ア
アン 安禪不必須山水滅却心頭火自涼 554

イ
イチ 一曲兩曲無人會雨過夜塘秋水深 521

ウ
ウン 雲開月色家家白春過山花處處紅 607

イチ 一口吸盡西江水洛陽牡丹新吐藥 516
イチ 一毫端現寶王刹微塵裏轉大法輪 519
イチ 一拶當機怒雷吼驚起須彌藏北斗 517
イチ 一種是聲無限意有堪聽與不堪聽 523
イチ 一樹春風有兩般南枝向暖北枝寒 522
イチ 一重山盡又一重話盡山雲海月情 527
イチ 一陣西風吹雨過夕陽總在海棠花 528
イチ 一段風流玉琢成一枝留得舊風流 518
イチ 一趯趯飜四大海一拳拳倒須彌山 526
イチ 一二三四五六七碧眼胡僧不知數 515
イチ 一片白雲橫谷口幾多歸鳥夜迷巢 520
イチ 一與山門作境致二與後人作標榜 525
イチ 一粒粟中藏世界半升鐺內煮山川 524

十方無虚空大地無寸土 （ジュウ）431
十年歸不得忘却來時道 （ジュウ）430
出門逢釋迦入門逢彌勒 （シュツ）429
春眠不覺曉處處聞啼鳥 （シュン）455
春色無高下花枝自短長 （シュン）456
松樹千年翠不入時人意 （ショウ）460
松無古今色竹有上下節 （ショウ）461
鐘聲來舊寺月色下新池 （ショウ）486
心隨萬境轉轉處實能幽 （シン）450
盡大地是藥那箇是自己 （ジン）474
水流元入海月落不離天 （スイ）466
隨流認得性無喜亦無憂 （ズイ）489
世尊不説説迦葉不聞聞 （セ）423

青山元不動白雲自去來 （セイ）491
清風拂明月明月拂清風 （セイ）469
相逢相不識共語不知名 （ソ）475
達磨不會禪夫子不知字 （タツ）483
長者長法身短者短法身 （チョウ）487
張三喫鐵棒李四忍疼痛 （チョウ）448
獨坐幽篁裡彈琴復長嘯 （ト）472
微風吹幽松近聽聲愈好 （ビ）449
不知何處寺風送鐘聲來 （フ）422

扶過斷橋水伴歸無月村 （フ）452
佛殿裏燒香山門頭合掌 （ブツ）425
無風荷葉動決定有魚行 （ム）470
夜來風雨聲花落知多少 （ヤ）439
野火燒不盡春風吹又生 （ヤ）484
來説是非者便是是非人 （ライ）426
流水寒山路深雲古寺鐘 （リュウ）468
兩頭俱截斷一劍倚天寒 （リョウ）428
林下十年夢湖邊一笑新 （リン）462
路逢達道人不將語默對 （ロ）482

十二字 （六言對）

爲萬物之根源作天地之太祖 （イ）506
一喝大地震動一棒須彌粉碎 （イチ）493
一切聲是佛聲一切色是佛色 （イチ）492
寒時寒殺闍梨熱時熱殺闍梨 （カン）499
求美則不得美不求美則美矣 （キュウ）504
去年貧未是貧今年貧始是貧 （キョ）495
近則不離方寸遠則十萬八千 （キン）510
坐斷千聖路頭打破群魔境界 （ザ）496

ヨ

要行便行要坐便坐 408

リ

李花不白桃花不紅 390

龍吟雲起虎嘯風生 417

十字 （五言対）

ア

庵中閑打坐白雲起峰頂 447

イ

已見寒梅發復聞啼鳥聲 446

一華開五葉結果自然成 420

一句定乾坤一劍平天下 418

一點梅花藥三千世界香 421

一峰雲片片雙澗水潺潺 419

陰陽不到處一片好風光 488

ウ

宇宙無雙日乾坤只一人 442

雲掩仲秋月雨打上元燈 490

玉向泥中潔松經雪後貞 473

カ

懷州牛喫禾益州馬腹張 451

寒雲抱幽石霜月照清池 443

キ

歸來坐虛室夕陽在吾西 465

掬水月在手弄花香滿衣 453

九夏寒岩雪三冬枯木花 424

泣露千般草吟風一樣松 467

牛飲水成乳蛇飲水成毒 471

行到水窮處坐看雲起時 480

金屑眼中翳衣珠法上塵 485

ク

空手把鋤頭步行騎水牛 477

君看此花枝中有風露香 437

薫風自南來殿閣生微涼 479

ケ

月知明月秋花知一樣春 458

月到中秋滿風從八月涼 457

月落潭無影雲生山有衣 459

コ

古松談般若幽鳥弄眞如 435

枯木倚寒巖三冬無暖氣 463

吾心似秋月碧潭清皎潔 436

好事不出門惡事行千里 440

兀然無事坐春來草自生 427

サ

坐水月道場修空華萬行 438

採菊東籬下悠然見南山 454

山花開似錦澗水湛如藍 445

山中無曆日寒盡不知年 444

シ

只許老胡知不許老胡會 434

只在此山中雲深不知處 433

此夜一輪滿清光何處無 464

始隨芳草去又逐落花回 441

詩向快人吟酒逢知己飲 481

終日走紅塵失却自家珍 478

秋風吹渭水落葉滿長安 476

十方薄伽梵一路涅槃門 432

八字

TERMINOLOGY, NAMES
AND OTHER CAPITALIZED WORDS

A 24
August 457

Barrier 540
Bhagavān 432
Big Dipper 215
  517
bodhi 629
Body 341 631
Buddha 154 235
  Hall 425
Buddhas 628

Cáo Wellspring
  195
Cháng-ān 183
Courage 202
Crow 399 566

December 338
Dharma 393
  Hall 479
  Wheel 519
Diamond King
  212
Dipper 215 517

Earth 617
East 116 123 307
  399 544 594
Eye 393

gkhaught!!! 8
Golden Body 631
  Crow 399 566
  Wind 176
Great Dharma
  Wheel 519
  Courage 202
  Táng 293
  Way 183
Gūsū city 570

hai! 7
Hall 425 479
Hán-shān-sì 570
Hare 399
Harmony 150
Heaven 428 617
ho! 10 106
Holy Ones 404

Jade Hare 399
Jasanrō 348
Jōshū 630

kanji 348
karma 87 89
Kāśyapa 423
King 212
kōan 315

Lasting Peace
  593
Lǐ 448
Longevity 593
Lù 539
Luòyáng 516

May 560 569
Mind 263 393
  628
Moon-faced 235
Mount Lù 539
Mount Sumeru
  517 526
mu! 14
my Way 228
Mystery 604

Nirvāna 393 432
North 544
NOT 173

One 228 407 423
  Mind 263
  Way 432

Patriarch 206
Patriarchs 154
Peace 593
Peak 202 550
  612 626
Penetralia of
  Mystery 604
Purity 150

Reverence 150
River 516 539
  560
  Xiāng 242

Self 584
Silla 293
Single Body 341
South 544
Sumeru 517 526
śunyatā 406
Sun-faced 235

Tán River 242
Táng 293
THIS 58 228 384
Thusness 435
Tokuun 626
Tranquillity 150
Truc Dharma
  393
  Nature 489

Way 183 187 228
  312 336 376 405
  432 482
Wellspring 195
West 116 123
  206 307 399 544
  556 589
  River 516
  Wheel 519
  Wind 176
  Wisdom 435
Wonder Peak
  626
World-honored
  423
Wǔlǎo Peak 550
Wǔtái 536

Xiāng 242
Xiānglú Peak
  612

Yáng Barrier
  540
Yíaì-sì 612

Zen 357
Zhāng 448
Zhé River 539

COMMON WORDS

able to 578
about 315
to 408
above 218 366
377
abuse 154
abyssal 133
accord with 413
according to 359
aching 448
across 520
act as 506
action 359 597
add 358
adhere 629
admiring 537
advice 598
after 368 473
509 521 561 571
605
rain 356
them 335
again 65 193 446
484 516
against 87 463
570
ages 100 576 584
agitated 305
ahead 80
air 438 442 623
alas! 9
alert 55 500
alight 191
alike 458 467
561
alive 484
all 261 298 334
509
alike 458 467
around 272
beings 189
kinds 467
lands 555
one 549 608
the more 589
things 506 617
-pervading 393

alone 202 377
472 628
along 472 552
with 441 568
already 346 446
538 587
also 254
altogether 571
always 491 560
ambience 571
amid 560
among 577
ancient 67 372
461 468 486 508
535
movement 518
temple 565
anciently 435
anew 605
angry fist 229
another 361 503
521 527 556 589
answer 100
anything 101
anyway 531
apart 549
ape 586
apes 538 585
appear 459 561
581
appearance 492
appears 519
apprehend 508
arising 351
around 322 573
arrow 286
as far as 604
ashen staff 574
ashy head 104
ass 221 306
ass! 3
astride 477 536
atop 618
attains 518
attentive 135
attentively 140
authority 587

autumn 270 445
457 458 534 594
dewdrops 284
heat 623
leaves 607
moon 490
-clear 521
awake 455
away 275 276
510 528 623
azure 611

back home 60
575
backward 536
bad deeds 440
ball 233
bamboo 357 454
461 530 562 573
577 592
grove 472
pole 558
bamboos 596
banks 538
bar 75
barbarian-monk
515
barrier 23
bars 405
battle 587
be clear 628
beads 485
beak 585
bear 523
bearded 251
bears 448
along 573
beat 502
beating 293
beats 290
beautiful 504
550
beauty 504 557
582
become 143 400
becomes 411 471

before 97 188
205 368 404 535
585 618
beg 91
begging-bag 79
beginningless
584
begun 613
behind 97 224
538 546 614
being 263
beings 189 366
bell 422 468 486
508 570 612
belly 451
below 218 366
532
beneath 392
besides 505
better 449
beyond 389 527
540 562 570 587
621
big 624
billows 618
bird 266 273 296
585
birds 435 446
455 520 563
birth 88 291
-and-death 584
bit 488 534
bitter 530 598
black 253
lacquer 82 134
363
blade of grass
631
blazing 630
blends with 149
blind 65 136 179
612
bloom 169 333
599
blooms 217
blossom 263

hands 453
hang out 234
happening on
410
happy 488
hard 289 553
swung 325
to 155
hardest 245
hare 256 260 498
harmony 141
harvest 436
has been no 368
got to be 371
hating 588
he 73 624
head 104 128
175 234 253 349
497 622
heads 428
in 574
heaped upon 351
hear 446 449 455
523 612 619
heard 423
hearing 396 423
508
hears 262
heartbroken 600
hearts 527
heat 499 623
heaven 207 217
230 270 292 298
377 442 543 572
587 616
heavens 191 268
418 570
heavenward 535
heavily 609
heavy 557
layers 559
held up 115
help carry 626
heralds 269
hidden 334
practice 395
hide 181 490
in 517
hiding 412

high 332 622
seas 526
-leaping 532
-minded 624
higher 614
hills 300 454
hoe 477
hold water 453
holds 585
up 555
hole 223
holes 245
holy 114 369
home 59 60 126
151 331 547 575
578 607
homeward 544
homing birds
520
honored 377
horizon 609
hornless 324
horns 260 601
621
horse 381 383
415 451 594
horsehead 247
host 112
house 147 281
347 478
household 249
how 367 505 630
to 515
however much
265
huge 258
hum 125 417
human life 604
108,000 510
hundred feet 332
-foot pole 591
hundreds 333
560
hunger comes
361 362
hunt 511
hut 447

I 377 600
eat 362

I laugh 339
say 346
sleep 362
ice 500
melts 144
idea 625
idiot 248
sages 626
ignorant 483
illumines 352
443
heaven 207
imbued 434
imbues 272
immensity 416
immersed 619
impeding 76
impenetrable
614
impenetrably 75
imperative 92
impermanence
630
importance 550
important 177
improves 598
in front 546
incense 425
inch 624
away 510
of land 295 431
incomplete 265
indeed 495
indicating 116
indigo 445
individual 509
inept 395
inexhaustibility
583
inexplainable 96
inferior 487
infinity 450
infused 483
innate 121
inside 524
insight 482
instant 359
intense light 327
intensely 521
still 586

intention 155
intersection 287
intimate friend
275 481
friends 335
invariably 274
inward 107
iron 289
bull 324
hammers 223
ox 259
rod 448
tree 169 354
wall 353
isles 541
itch 166
itself 427
ivied window
595

jade-white 256
-green 436
jeweled staff 616
sword 212
joints 461
joy 489 627
jump about 298
jumps about 216
just being on 263
like 316
listening 600
one call 266

keen man 383
keep on 375
smiling 549
keeps company
452
kick over 388
up 526
kill 410
kills 243 499
kind 523
knock over 526
know 32 49 94
270 335 439 508
529 594 621 628
each other 316
how to 515
when 48

ordinary 615
mind 187
original 509
orioles 569
other 626
others 523 613
ourselves 523
out of 589
of touch 276
of place 380
with 624
outside 382
over 444 447 535
541 609 610
overhead 416
owl-old 566
own 628
ox 259 451 621
-head 247

pagoda 583
pail 82 134 257
363
pain 280 448
painted at 265
painting 578
pair 613
palace 586
pale moon 573
palm 503
paradise 541
part 291 607
partridge 560
579
pass 617
in 381
passes 607
passing 470 625
past 529 621 628
path 468 496
peace 110
peaceful 554
peach 392
blossoms 240
318 390
peak 419 447
606 618 622
peaks 214 542
544 585

pear blossoms
610
peck 105
pelts 490 610
peonies 516
people 574 627
perfect 223 405
disc 611
perfection 518
perfectly reveals
360
petal 556 589
petals 420 610
petty 624
phrase 404
pick up 303
out 304
pierces 596
pilgrim boat 570
pillar 170 227
pillow 588 612
pinch up 295 551
pine 449 473 555
562 605 609
trees 460
wind 244
-old 391
-trees 197
pines 357 435
461 467 595
pink 390
pissing 113 535
pivot 322
place 159 199
204 334 413 431
464 509 545
plain 594
plantain leaves
600
planting 530 599
plastered 531
plays to 264
plum 446 556
557 571
blossom 263
blossoms 240
390 533
trees 392 530
573
twigs 572

plum-blossom
421
poem 344 481
593 603
poet 603
point 116 545
points 285
right at 400
pole 332 558 591
620
polished 518
pool 372 436 443
459 486 532 596
pools 521 581
possible 344
pot 182 550
pottery frag-
ments 303
poverty 495 545
practice 371 395
438
further 41
preach 357
precious 411
precipice 463
preferences 405
presence 508
present 529 628
colors 461
event 143
presses down
609
prevails 587
privately 381
probing staff 117
produces 258
479
profound 576
profoundly 435
profusion 313
progenitor 506
prominently 349
pull 222
punishment 109
pure breeze 267
body 186 582
gold 343
light 464
white 436
push aside 118

put down 575
on 355 361
puts atop 175
to fright 339

quakes 493
quarter-hours 72
questions 630
quick 256 481
quietly 563

raccoon dog 327
529
radishes 258
raging thunder
517
rain 238 272 337
356 357 370 439
490 528 539 600
610
rainy 226
raised 559
range 527
rank 137 178
536
rapids 233
ravine 520
reach 488 549
553
reached 310
reaching 570
readiness of time
501
real 401 495
nature 628
realization 371
realize 384 489
605
really 15 523
realm 282 494
realms 365
recitation 344
recluse 533
recognizing 475
red 124 240 241
320 566 575
dust 478
flags 152
redder 537
reed flowers 308